The Bible

Beyond the Impasse

HIGHLAND
LOCH PRESS

The Bible

Beyond the Impasse

William J. Abraham

Highland Loch Press
Dallas, Texas, USA

To Ivan Abraham

Front Design by Darryl Lilly
of Wordsmith Media, Inc.

First edition
Published by Highland Loch Press
Dallas, Texas, USA
in association with
Wordsmith Academic Press

ISBN-10: 0985310235
ISBN-13: 978-0-9853102-3-3

www.highlandlochpress.com

Contents

Preface

This little volume constitutes the content of the Heck lectures delivered at United Theological Seminary in Dayton, Ohio, on April 10-11, 2007. I am extremely grateful to Dean Wendy J. Deichman Edwards for the kind invitation to give these lectures and for the wonderful hospitality given to me during my stay at United Seminary. President J. Edwin Zeiders was a splendid host. I could not have asked for a better reception from the perceptive and alert faculty of United Seminary and from the students and guests who attended the lectures. In preparing the lectures for publication the changes I have made are essentially cosmetic. The first lecture was also presented as a paper at the *Hermeneutics and Scripture Consultation* at Baylor University, June 1-3, 2006, and was subsequently published as a chapter in David L. Jeffrey and C. Stephan Evans (eds.), *The Bible and the University*, under the title, *Scripture in Christian Theology*.[1] I am grateful to the participants at that consultation for their spirited response. I have also added

---

[1] David L. Jeffrey and C. Stephan Evans (eds.), *The Bible and the University* (Grand Rapids, Mich: Zondervan, 2007).

some remarks and footnotes and an epilogue to fill out the lectures that were originally given.

The material here does not represent a full-scale vision of scripture and its place in the life of the church, but it does indicate the core of what I think is needed for an apt and spiritually nourishing vision of scripture for our day and time.

1. The Authority of Scripture and the Birth of Biblical Theology

We are now in a crisis that no individual can measure, nor his piety deal with; and it is beyond any philosophy or idealism of a time. It needs the faith of an agelong holy Church to grasp it. Would that the Church's faith could always handle it in the true power of the crisis greater still which made the Church – in the power of the Church's Cross and Gospel. An awful crisis of wickedness like this war can only be met on the Church's height and range of faith; and it forces us up to levels and aspects of our belief which our common hours of moral slackness too easily feel extreme. Nothing but the great theologies of redemption are adequate to the great tragedies of the world.

P. T. Forsyth.[2]

Introduction: An Important Platitude

It is a platitude in Christian theology that scripture plays a pivotal role in the origins and warrants of Christian doctrine. Until the modern period, this platitude was pretty much central to the heartbeat of theology in the

---

[2] Peter Taylor Forsyth, *The Justification of God: Lectures for War-Time on a Christian Theodicy* (London: Duckworth, 1916), 128.

West, that is, in both Protestant and Catholic theology. To raise questions about this basic epistemological assumption, that scripture is the crucial if not the only norm of Christian theology, was to be outside the pale.

This disposition to look to scripture as a foundation for theology fitted nicely with an epistemological conception of scripture. Scripture was read first and foremost as both the source and norm of Christian theological proposals. The very sense of canon was articulated in terms of scripture being a criterion; and scripture also fixed the reference for canon, in that canon was constituted by scripture. This did not preclude appeal to other epistemic norms like, say, tradition; but tradition was carefully subordinated to the canon of scripture even in those communities that gave a high place to tradition. Effectively tradition was a hermeneutical norm for getting at the meaning of scripture.[3]

To be sure, other sorts of readings were permitted so that one could read scripture for devotional purposes, seek in scripture food for

---

[3] This was, of course, a dead-end, requiring in the Roman Catholic tradition the development of papal infallibility as a way of resolving disputes between rival interpretive traditions.

the soul, encouragement for the journey of faith, or comfort in sorrow. Indeed it was impossible to eliminate such appropriations of scripture because, after all, scripture is the foundational text for Christian preaching. Preaching necessarily has devotional overtones and aims; preaching is not simply lecturing; it is a practice aimed at cultivating the life of faith. Yet, as can be seen in the longstanding polemic against allegorical readings of scripture and against pietism, such readings were often frowned upon; at the very least it was thought that devotional and homiletical usage of scripture should presuppose a literal sense of scripture as the normative foundation for Christian faith and practice. To this end theologians created the discipline of biblical studies in order to ensure that the foundational work on which they relied was executed with proper skill and care.

The Creation of Biblical Studies

An epistemological vision of scripture has clearly shaped the curricula of Protestant schools of theology. In the Reformed, Lutheran, and Anglican tradition it was agreed that one should begin one's theological studies by learning the relevant original languages and then settle into a detailed study of the scriptural texts. The result was the founding of intellectual disciplines devoted to a book. So we have chairs of Biblical Studies, of the Interpretation of Scripture, of the Old and New Testaments, of Biblical Languages, of Biblical Theology, and so on. It is surely odd in the extreme that we have professors of a book (the bible), or even parts of a book (the New Testament or the Old Testament). Yet it strikes no-one as incongruous that this is the case, for the oddity made sense in a theological world where the initial and indispensable work in Christian theology lay in the careful study of scripture conceived as a norm that gave us access to the full range of truth about God and everything else insofar as it related to God. Other disciplines in the world of theological encyclopedia, that is, church history, systematic theology, practical theology, and the like, were always secondary if not parasitic to biblical studies. Some sub-disciplines, like philosophical theology, were entirely optional; indeed philosophical theology might well be treated with hostility because it can readily become a rival "fundamental theology", where issues of norm are treated as lying outside the purview of biblical studies.

The epistemological place of biblical studies was confirmed by the ready place given to scripture by systematic theology. Indeed over time the loci of systematic theology were expanded to include complex *prolegomena* whose primary purpose was to lay out and defend a vision of scripture as the critical norm for all theology. This looks straightforward on the surface; after all, the task of the systematic theologian lies on the other side of biblical studies, so let each be done in its own time and season. However, this leaves systematic theology unstable and secondary. The theologian must not only await the findings of biblical studies but also be constantly prepared to revise the content of their systematic theology. Clearly this leaves the structure and content of systematic theology up for grabs. Theology must now come to terms with a permanent revolution in its domain.

My favorite piece of evidence for this enduring disruption within theology is the impassioned plea that shows up in the Scottish tradition. I invite the reader to pause and ponder what might happen if we were to follow the mandate of the hardy writers of the Scot's Confession (1560).

> …if any man will note in our Confession any chapter or sentence contrary to God's Holy Word, that it would please

him of his gentleness and for Christian charity's sake to inform us of it in writing; and we, upon our honor, do promise him that by God's grace we shall give him satisfaction from the mouth of God, that is, from Holy Scripture, or else we shall hereafter alter whatever he can prove to be wrong.[4]

Roman Catholic scholars have at times relished the enduring disruption that has ensued across the history of modern and postmodern thought as a result of this strategy. As Brad S. Gregory has recently made manifest, it is relatively easy to hammer away at the intellectual disasters that have been engendered by the appeal to scripture alone. In his brilliant *tour de force, The Unintended Reformation,*[5] he charted, with both pleasing elegance and magnificent documentation, the fascinating outcome of this revolutionary development. What he has

---

[4] Quoted in B. A. Gerrish, *Saving and Secular Faith: An Invitation to Systematic Theology* (Minneapolis, MN: Fortress Press, 1999), 61.

[5] Brad S. Gregory, *The Unintended Reformation, How a Religious Revolution Secularized Society* (Cambridge, Mass.: The Belknap Press of Harvard University Press, 2012). Despite its conceptual and historical limitations, this volume is essential reading for charting a future for any robust vision of Christianity in the future.

failed to see is that the doctrine of *sola scriptura* was alive and well in Aquinas, and even before that, in various early Fathers. To that extent the story must begin a lot earlier than where he locates its origins. Even more importantly, he is blind to the fact that the move to treat scripture in epistemic categories is central to the cause he champions, namely, those churches over which the Bishop of Rome has sought to exercise authority. The crucial issue is not simply the move to derive everything from scripture; it is the move to reduce the rich canonical heritage of the church to scripture, and then to insist on making epistemology the critical factor in understanding Christianity. Gregory has conveniently ignored the alternative options available in the early tradition and the alternative trajectory that has worked itself out in the East.

Initially the acute difficulty that the appeal to *sola scriptura* introduces into theology can readily be concealed. So long as biblical scholars buy into the favored creedal or confessional commitments of the day, biblical scholars and systematic theologians can paper over the revolutionary consequences of an epistemic conception of scripture for centuries. However, once a serious clash between biblical scholars and theologians arises, the cat is out of the bag, and it is always going to be a challenge to catch her and put her firmly back in place. Cats are, after all, promiscuous and elusive by nature.

In reality modern biblical studies arose as a massive effort to get free of the strictures of systematic theology. Systematic theology came to be seen as a narrow-minded parent that undercut the freedom of the biblical scholar. Happily, the rebellious children could stave off criticism by appealing to a core conviction of the parents, for biblical scholarship was set up by theology in the first place precisely to discover the content of scripture. The core problem for biblical scholarship was this: systematic theology was seen as imposing constraints that undercut the proper study and place of scripture in Christian theology. The constraints were of two radically different kinds. One constraint was derived from theories of inspiration that required that the study of scripture be read with a hermeneutic of epistemic generosity, that is, that scripture be read, say, as historically, morally, and theologically inerrant, infallible, reliable, or in some other praiseworthy manner. A second and very different constraint was that scripture be read in such a way as to underwrite the ancient creedal faith of the church or of the pertinent confessions of various modern Christian denominations. So biblical scholars came under suspicion if their findings were incompatible with this or that first-order vision of Christian theology. Yet Christian theology itself required that biblical studies be primary, so biblical scholars had theology itself on their side; they were simply carrying out the academic mandate set for them by an epistemic vision of their materials. Thus from the beginning it was clear that biblical scholarship had the upper hand in the debate with theology; theologians by their own canons of thinking had agreed on the foundational nature of scripture, so those who studied scripture had to be given the first if not the last word in theology.

The Unexpected Disaster

It would be tedious and beyond my competence to unpack the story that unfolded within the horizon I have just sketched.[6] The

---

[6] James Barr's *The Concept of Biblical Theology: An Old Testament Perspective* (Minneapolis, MN: Fortress Press, 1999) is a landmark study, the fruit of a lifetime's ruminations. Michael C. Legaspi, *The Death of Scripture and the Rise of Biblical Studies* (New York: Oxford University Press, 2010) is also worth consulting.

hopes engendered by the rise of biblical studies as a logically distinct but not separate sub-discipline within theological studies require a creative act of imagination if they are to be appreciated. Nowhere was this clearer than within Protestantism where the scholarly industry in and around scripture has been so impressive. The end result, however, has been disastrous for theology. The outcome is now clear: biblical studies no longer acts as a feeder discipline for theology. It has become a region of expertise on its own that is carefully guarded by the scholarly guilds. It is rare in the extreme for a theologian to be allowed to teach a course on scripture; in most cases theologians would refuse that option where it given them. More importantly, there are simply no secure results that the theologian can now rely on in the foundations of his or her work. We simply have a Babel of voices in the guild; and theologians are in no position to adjudicate the alternatives.

Karl Rahner captures the crisis cleanly.

> When you [biblical exegetes] simply leave the work of bridging the gap between exegesis and dogmatic theology conveniently to us, and we poor dogmatic theologians want to take up this work (and have then to concern

ourselves also with exegesis, since a bridge crosses from one bank to another) then you are the first to shout – admit it – that we dogmatic theologians understand nothing about exegesis, and that it would be far better if we left it alone rather than dabbling in it in a clumsy sort of way! Who then is to do this job that must be done? You behave rather strangely sometimes in this matter. On the one hand, you complain that too little attention is being paid to the Scriptures, that there is too much scholastic theology and not enough biblical theology. But then, when it comes to the point where it would be necessary to show how and where in the Scriptures the Church's teaching finds its expression or at least its ultimate basis, you begin to excuse yourselves and declare that even with the best will in the world you cannot find anything in the Scripture which would serve as a basis for the teaching of the Church.[7]

The general situation is, of course, complicated, but we should note two factors that confound the dilemma. First, in the

[7] Karl Rahner, 'Exegesis and Dogmatic Theology,' in *Theological Investigations, Vol. 5* (London: Darton, Longman & Todd, 1966), 71-72.

modern period of biblical studies the drive to read the text as functional atheists is very powerful. In order to be truly academic, historical, *wissenschaftlich*, critical, and the like, students of scripture had to bracket their theistic and confessional commitments.[8] To be sure, this was more of an ideal than a reality. Many scholars, the likes of Martin Kähler and Adolf Schlatter in Germany, or the disciples of the great trio, J. B. Lightfoot, B. F. Westcott, and F. J. A. Hort in Britain, never bought this line.[9] Moreover, most scholars have been practicing Christians and have gone about their work both motivated and informed by their faith. Yet the general reality has been that scripture scholars methodologically have had to describe and explain the phenomena of the text as if God does not exist. Anyone who challenged this, like Brevard S. Childs in the last generation, has had to construct a massive counter-paradigm that trades on theological convictions that are inevitably contested and

---

[8] For a spirited reiteration of this tradition see Jacques Berlinerblau, *The Secular Bible, Why Nonbelievers Must Take Religion Seriously* (Cambridge: Cambridge University Press, 2005).

[9] For the latter, see Stephen C. Neill and Tom Wright, *The Interpretation of the New Testament: 1861-1986* (Oxford: Oxford Univ. Press, 1989).

controversial.[10] In any case, internal differences along theological lines simply made matters worse by increasing the number and voices in Babel. In reality biblical scholars have diverged both on the method and results of their work from the beginning.

Second, with the rise of postmodernism in biblical scholarship the old ideal developed by figures like Ernst Troeltsch and Van Harvey has come under heavy fire.[11] The tendency now is to celebrate the diversity of voices with gusto and thus to make a virtue out of necessity. Indeed the old ideal is vigorously attacked for its sham self-criticism, in that its claims to neutrality and objectivity are interpreted as power-plays that mask the discriminatory racist, classist, and sexist

[10] The contested and partisan character of Childs's position becomes patently clear in Paul G. McGlasson's *Invitation to Dogmatic Theology: A Canonical Approach* (Grand Rapids, Mich.: Brazos Press, 2006), a text endorsed with enthusiasm by Childs himself. What McGlasson in reality wants to propose is a revisionary return to *sola scriptura*, with Augustine, Barth, and Childs operating as a privileged canon of theologians who provide the horizon for scriptural interpretation.

[11] Van Harvey provided a brilliant restatement of Troeltsch in his *The Historian and the Believer: The Morality of Historical Knowledge and Christian Belief* (Urbana: University of Illinois Press, 1996). This was originally published by Macmillan, in New York, in 1966.

impulses that lie below the surface. Thus the very idea of looking for any kind of stable meaning in the text is excoriated. Ironically, the editors of *The Postmodern Bible* make the point with pleasing clarity when they explain the title of their work in terms of shared

> suspicion of the claim to mastery that characterizes traditional reading of texts, including modern biblical scholarship …by sweeping away secure notions of meaning, by radically calling into question the apparently stable foundations of meaning on which traditional interpretation is situated, by raising doubts about the capacity to achieve ultimate clarity about the meaning of a text, postmodern readings lay bare the contingent and constructed character of meaning itself.[12]

So, where once it was at least assumed that there were texts with stable authors and meanings to be understood, this assumption is now under suspicion, if not completely rejected.[13]

---

[12] *The Postmodern Bible: The Bible and Culture Collective* (New Haven: Yale University Press, 1995), 2-3.
[13] It is interesting that even John J. Collins, one of the great contemporary champions of "historical criticism", feels

There is, of course, an easy solution to the dilemma I have sketched which is immediately open to the theologian. Let the theologian join the ranks of postmodernism and develop a theology to fit the new data emanating from the guild of biblical scholarship.[14] What is interesting about this response is how modern and traditional it is. It buys into the traditional assumption that scripture is foundational for theology, for this provides the warrant for taking the current orthodoxy in biblical studies seriously; and it accepts the modern assumption that the task of theology is to take the findings of biblical scholarship and move from there to a theology that will be credible in the light of the epistemological regime of the day. What is

---

under pressure to deal with the postmodernist crusade against meaning. See his exceptionally interesting *The Bible after Babel: Historical Criticism in a Postmodern Age* (Grand Rapids, Mich: W. B. Eerdmans Pub. Co, 2005).

[14] Interestingly there is both a conservative and radical way to make this move. Thus conservatives have turned to postmodernity as a way to reinscribe their confessional commitments in biblical study; some, like the Pentecostals, have cleverly made hay of their marginal and oppressed status as their ticket to a seat at the table. The radical alternative is not to find a niche inside diversity but to revel in the reality of diversity as something intrinsically beautiful.

trumpeted as new and cutting edge is in fact old, stale, and suffocating.

The Really Deep Problem

I have not, however, hit bottom yet. The deep problem that has befallen us is not the cacophony of voices that render the faith hopelessly unstable and erratic, giving it a shelf life of a generation or two. The real deep disaster is the loss of the gospel in the church.

It is hard to know how to state what I have in mind here succinctly and persuasively; it will suffice to make two points. First, the good news of the arrival of God's kingdom in the life, death, and resurrection of Jesus Christ through the working of the Holy Spirit is simply drowned in a sea of conflicting opinion. The gospel rather than being the radical, transforming Word of God becomes simply one more option among others. In this context the kind of fierce confidence that Paul displays in the first chapter of Galatians comes across as hopelessly dogmatic and intolerant. Second, any formation that takes place involves initiation into an arbitrary, parochial, sectarian version of Christianity rather than into an ecclesial vision of the Christian faith. At precisely a time when the church needs to recover its evangelistic nerve, scripture studies and theology together offer a variety of exotic stones when the convert looks for bread. At a time in Western culture when the church needs a trumpet sound she shows up in public as a noisy brass band whose members play from radically different scores. At a time when the church has learned to take seriously the seeker, she has nothing to offer but the satisfaction of spiritually untutored desire.

We have reached the end of an era in Protestantism where both scripture and theology are concerned. Theologians innocently created biblical studies as the foundation of their own work; biblical studies then undermined theology from within by systematically cutting theology off from its constitutive norm; both biblical studies and theology then in turn undermined access to the gospel for the ordinary believer. It is no surprise that in these circumstances varieties of Fundamentalism, Evangelicalism, and Pentecostalism continue to flourish within Western Protestantism. The popular preachers of these expanding movements have found a way to speak to the felt needs of people with an air of scriptural authority. Ironically there is a strange symbiotic relationship between these traditions and biblical studies, in that they provide much of the motivation and cognitive dissonance that fuels the continuation of biblical studies in the academy.[15] We have a bizarre self-destructive dance in which theologically motivated, epistemic conceptions of scripture drive Christians to engage in intellectual work that undermines both theology and personal faith from within.

Retracing Our Steps

By this stage some readers will have already begun to tune out. They will be tempted to dismiss what I have proposed as apocalyptic rather than sober, as exaggerated rather than accurate. So let me approach my concerns from a different angle. I propose to go back towards the origins of biblical studies and revisit a manifesto that casts light on our current difficulties. The advantage of this strategy is that it also allows me to indicate both the central problems I want to highlight and where we may have gone wrong. I have in

---

[15] A nice example is the recent work of Bart D. Ehrman who was driven to biblical studies by his fundamentalism and is spending a career sorting out what to do in biblical studies after losing his faith. See *Misquoting Jesus: The Story Behind who Changed the Bible and Why* (New York: HarperSanFrancisco, 2005).

mind returning to the remarkable inaugural address of J. P. Gabler given in 1784.[16] James Barr notes that Gabler's inaugural address is often mentioned but seldom read.[17] My intuition is that Gabler captures a crucial turning point in the discussion; we can readily detect in his work precisely the assumptions that took us down the wrong track.[18] Once articulated I can then lay out the changes that are essential for the future of theology and its relationship to scripture. To anticipate, I shall argue that what theology mistakenly gave away, she can now take back, and that she can do this without ignoring the incredible gains to be garnered from the historical study of scripture.[19] However, the retrieval of scripture, if it is to avoid the vain repetition of

[16] In J. P. Gabler's "An Oration on the Proper Distinction between Biblical and Dogmatic Theology and the Specific Objectives of Each." See John Sandys-Wunsch and Laurence Eldredge, "J. P. Gabler and the Distinction between Biblical and Dogmatic Theology: Translation, Commentary, and Discussion of His Originality," *Scottish Journal of Theology, Vol. 33,* 133-158.

[17] Barr, *Concept of Biblical Theology*, 642, footnote 16.

[18] How far Gabler's work has been historically influential need not be decided here.

[19] I use the soft term "historical study" rather than the term "historical criticism" in order to signal that I am well aware of the contested character of the latter. As we shall see, we need to make deflationary moves all along the line in our future work.

the modern and postmodern periods will require radical changes in the vision of scripture deployed, the scope of the canon, and the task of theology itself.

The problem that Gabler set out to resolve is one that is familiar to all acquainted with the history of scriptural interpretation, namely, that there is little agreement on what scripture actually teaches. Nobody would be bothered with this if we were dealing with any other canon of texts, but in the case of scripture this is disastrous given the normative status attributed to scripture in theology. Gabler opens his address with as good a statement of this normative dimension of the discussion as any.

> All who are devoted to the sacred faith of Christianity, most worthy listeners, profess with one united voice that the sacred books, especially of the New Testament, are the one clear source from which all true knowledge of the Christian religion is drawn. And they profess too that these books are the only secure sanctuary to which we can flee in the face of the ambiguity and vicissitude of human knowledge, if we aspire to a solid understanding of divine matters and if

we wish to obtain a firm and certain hope of salvation.[20]

The problem, of course, is that despite this agreement there is contention. "Why these fatal discords of the various sects?"[21] Gabler explains this discord along four lines. Scripture is often obscure; people read their own opinions into the text; folk do not distinguish between religion and theology; and, if they do, the problem arises "from an inappropriate combination of the simplicity and ease of biblical theology with the subtlety and difficulty of dogmatic theology."[22]

The problem that Gabler has identified is nothing new in Protestantism, for it was there from the beginning of the Reformation and was the cause of endless intellectual and

[20] Sandys-Wunsch and Eldredge, "J. P. Gabler and the Distinction between Biblical and Dogmatic Theology," 134. It is astonishing how readily Gabler is treated as an Enlightenment rationalist in the secondary literature.
[21] Ibid.
[22] Ibid., 135. It is crucial to note that Gabler takes divine revelation and divine inspiration with radical seriousness. He is clearly trying to nuance these notions in ways that will take into account God's accommodation to the needs of the times and to allow for genuine human action in the case of divine inspiration. Both these moves assume a hearty commitment to both divine revelation and divine inspiration.

political trouble in Europe for centuries. In the nineteenth century it haunted brilliant, sensitive souls like John Henry Newman and John Williamson Nevin, causing them theological and spiritual burnout for years before they found a way through it.[23] Gabler shows no signs of being haunted or suffering from burnout. He is confident that there is a clear way forward. His solution involves tackling the four sources of disagreement already identified. I shall begin with the last two and then look briefly at the first two.

One element in the solution is to get clear on the distinction between religion and theology.

> ...religion is passed on by the doctrine in the Scriptures, teaching what each Christian ought to know and believe and do in order to secure happiness in this life and in the life to come. Religion, then, is every-day, transparently clear

---

[23] Newman's agony is well captured in his *Apologia Pro Vita Sua: Being a History of His Religious Opinions* (London: Longmans, Green, Reader, and Dyer, 1875). Nevin provides a searing and devastating critique of North American Protestantism in his *Antichrist, or, The Spirit of Sect and Schism* (New York: J. S. Taylor, 1848). Nevin took five years to figure out whether he should or should not swim the Tiber; in the end, unlike Newman, he did not.

knowledge; but theology is subtle, learned knowledge, surrounded by a retinue of many disciplines, and by the same token derived not only from the sacred Scripture but also from elsewhere, especially from the domain of philosophy and history. It is therefore a field elaborated by human discipline and ingenuity. It is also a field that is advanced by careful and discriminating observation that experiences various changes along with other fields. Not only does theology deal with things proper to the Christian religion, but it also explains carefully and fully all connected matters; and finally it makes a place for them with the subtlety and rigor of logic. But religion for the common man has nothing to do with this abundance of literature and history.[24]

It is important to note here that Gabler is not in any way disparaging theology; on the contrary he sees it as essential to the Christian faith; and he intimates that it is a field of study not to be undertaken by the fainthearted who have no time for subtlety, learned knowledge, philosophy, history, and the rigor of logic. Yet

---

[24] Sandys-Wunsch and Eldredge, "J. P. Gabler and the Distinction between Biblical and Dogmatic Theology," 136.

Gabler rightly notes that there is something spiritually unsettling about this for the ordinary believer. In the end this kind of work can only be for the intellectually elite. Moreover, given its nature, it is inevitably marked by the idiosyncrasies and culturally relative situations of the theologian. Theology has a history and a chronology, where we move from the discipline of the Fathers to the scholastic theology of the Middle Ages, covered with the thick gloom of barbarity, to the light of the doctrine of salvation at the Reformation, on to the Socinian and Arminian factions of later times. Even within the Lutheran Church alone we can see a plethora of voices.

Gabler has surely put his finger on a critical problem, one that is readily dismissed today by theological rants about the easy simplicities and the cheap, vulgar certainties of Fundamentalism. The problem is simply that ordinary (and not so ordinary) people turn to Christianity looking for salvation, for hope, for a way forward in the darkness, for happiness in this life and in the life to come. If they turn to theology, they will soon be swamped by the ephemeral and changing judgments of the theologians. We might say that theology has become soteriologically dysfunctional; rather than give us food for the soul it offers elaborate menus and recipes; rather than lead us to God it leads into theological studies.

Gabler's solution is to offer the seeking soul not theology but religion. Here they can find the simplicity they rightly desire. More formally, what is needed is not dogmatic theology but biblical theology, a form of inquiry marked by "simplicity and ease". So religion and biblical theology are the solution to the difficultly thrown up by dogmatic theology. In addition the biblical theologian can provide an invaluable service to the dogmatic theologian by identifying material from scripture that is the foundation for their subtle, complex, rigorous work. The crux of the proposal is this:

> ...we distinguish carefully the divine from the human, that we establish some distinction between biblical and dogmatic theology, and after we have separated those things which in the sacred books refer most immediately to their own times and to the men of those times from those pure notions which divine providence wished to be characteristic of all times and places, let us then construct the foundation of our philosophy upon religion and let us designate with some care the objectives

27

of divine and human wisdom. Exactly thus will our theology be made more certain and more firm, and there will be nothing further to be feared for it from the most savage attack from its enemies.[25]

We have already crossed over into Gabler's solution to the first two problems we mentioned above, namely, the problem of obscurity and of eisegesis. We are also beginning to sense that a mushy bog is beginning to show up beneath our feet, for it is beginning to look as if the simplicity of biblical theology is a highly qualified simplicity. What we now want to know is how to get access to religion by the method of biblical as opposed to dogmatic theology.

Happily, Gabler hammers on undaunted. What is needed is a comprehensive study of scripture that will use the relevant philological skills, make appropriate distinctions between the Old and New Testament, put each author in the proper period, pay attention to the reflection of time and place, look at whether we are dealing with historical or didactic or poetic material, read below the surface of the

[25] Sandys-Wunsch and Eldredge, "J. P. Gabler and the Distinction between Biblical and Dogmatic Theology," 138.

text, sort out mention of an idea from proof of an idea, and so on. Clearly this whole operation is replete with a network of challenges in and around these issues and at every step along the way. We must then add to this a second challenge, namely, the task of sorting through this wealth of material and finding what is universal across the differences. "…each single opinion must be examined for its universal ideas, especially for those which are expressly read in this or that place in the Holy Scriptures, but according to this rule: that each of the ideas is consistent with its own era, its own testament, its own place of origin, and its own genius."[26] Once this is done, "…then finally there will be the happy appearance of biblical theology, pure and unmixed with foreign things, and we shall at last have the sort of system for biblical theology that Tiedmann elaborated with such distinction for Stoic philosophy."[27]

Karl Rahner should now be happy. The theologian is off the hook on exegesis for it has been handed to him by biblical theology. Gabler will be happy too. As he notes:

[26]Sandys-Wunsch and Eldredge, "J. P. Gabler and the Distinction between Biblical and Dogmatic Theology," 141-2.
[27] Ibid.

...as soon as all these things have been properly observed and carefully arranged, at last a clear sacred Scripture will be selected with scarcely any doubtful readings, made up of passages which are appropriate to the Christian religion of all times. These passages will show with unambiguous words the form of faith that is truly divine; the *dicta classica* properly so called, which can then be laid out as the fundamental basis for a more subtle, dogmatic scrutiny.[28]

And what are the tasks of the dogmatic theologian at that point? Gabler mentions two. First, the theologian works out a harmony between the findings of scripture and the principles of human reason.[29] Second, the theologian elaborates on the fundamentals supplied by biblical theology, "according to the variety both of philosophy and of every

[28] Ibid., 143. The "*dicta classica*" are the new proof texts for systematic theology. Gabler's traditionalist underwear is in full view at this point.

[29] This is no doubt why Gabler is so easily treated as a terrible rationalist of the Enlightenment, but seeking harmony between the truths of scripture and reason is a long-standing practice in Christian theology that cannot be confined to the dark days of the Enlightenment. It is also surely intrinsic to any serious theology.

human point of view of that which is subtle, learned, suitable and appropriate, elegant and graceful…"[30]

Back to the Crisis Again

In reviewing Gabler from our current situation it is clear that his solution, however creative and fruitful it may have been in the history of biblical scholarship, does not solve the problems he set out to resolve. The obscurity of scripture remains, as does the constant danger of reading our own opinions into the text.[31] The methodological flaw represented by the distinction between religion and theology is obvious on its face. Biblical theology turns out to be utterly similar to dogmatic theology in that it also involves a host of skills, materials, practices, and ancillary disciplines. So the simplicity at this

---

[30] Ibid., 144.

[31] It is currently hoped that reading the text from the underside or from the margins will save the day at this point; this too is a forlorn hope, as we can see when we note how this kind of reading so readily fits with and is generated by the prior political and theological commitments of its proponents. Of course, it is always possible for biblical scholars to see through all this and still learn to play this game with great sophistication and concealment.

level is a chimera.[32] So too is the simplicity by way of results: we are confronted with the same sort of development, difference, and diversity that has cropped up in the history of theology. Biblical studies, like theology, has a chronology and a history. Moreover, if we take Gabler's results, we will have already cooked the theological books in advance, for Gabler has in fact committed himself theologically in the way he handles the canon of scripture itself.[33] To put the matter technically, Gabler has in fact elected for a

---

[32] Yet the ideal dies hard. Consider the requirements for an educated clergy laid out by Paul C. McGlasson. "That education must include full proficiency in Greek and Hebrew; a complete grasp of church history in its setting in world history; comprehensive training in the canonical shape of both Testaments of scripture; firm grounding in biblical and dogmatic theology; wide exposure to the history and contemporary work of biblical exegesis; practical training in the art of pastoral care; and genuine understanding of the mission of the church in the world." See his *Invitation to Dogmatic Theology, A Canonical Approach*, 158. Amazingly, given McGlasson's emphasis on preaching, not a word is said about homiletics. However, what is really interesting is that the norm articulated here (even if we take it as a counsel of perfection) is a recipe for intellectual and theological self-deception and illusion.

[33] Of course, the whole enterprise depends on theology for it is the church and theology that supplies the scripture in the first place. The tortured contortions on what to call the Old Testament ("Hebrew Scripture", "The First Testament") makes this point all too clear.

vision of canon within the canon in his interpretation of scripture. Thus his goal is to unearth by painstaking exegetical and historical work the universal ideas that can be extracted from scripture. This is where he lands when he sets out to find the unambiguous, clear, certain, undoubted, fundamentally appropriate teaching of scripture that the theologian is to carry back to the office.

Thus Gabler in the end brings us right back to where we started. By its own intentions theology created biblical studies in order to carry out the first, foundational phase of its work. Biblical scholarship gladly took on the service for which it was created; but in time such scholarship took on a life of its own, becoming a field of inquiry that could neither in principle nor in practice deliver the goods. We might say that biblical studies is no longer in the business of taking orders from the theology department; thus theology by setting up scripture as its canon of truth has inevitably self-destructed from within. While theologians may still send in orders to the Biblical Studies Department, the orders are no longer being filled in or dispatched. The theologians in handing over their scriptures to biblical scholars have lost their scriptures, and thus, by their own norm, they are bereft of the resources they identified as constitutive of their work.

It is the spiritual effects of this development that are truly devastating. Where before we had sects of theology, we now have sects of biblical studies. And while the sects multiply, those who seek after God are left wandering on the hills without help for their souls. The gospel is now swamped by experts in biblical studies as much as by experts in theology. In Gabler's terms, there is no religion to which the hungry soul can turn. Spiritual darkness and hopeless insecurity have enveloped all of us on this side of Enlightenment. Distrust, suspicion, anomie, boredom, one-upmanship, and dogmatism stalk the theological landscape.

The effects of this on theological students can be fascinating to behold. Some simply drop out and turn, say, to neuroscience as a way out of the mess. They buy the standard atheistic or secular line that theology is a bankrupt discipline and that the way to achieve their aim of making a real difference in the world (they retain a secularized optimism of grace) is to turn to a cutting edge new science. Others retreat into a favored dogmatism of the past, most conspicuously adopting a hardline version of Calvinism or Barthianism and settle in for the long journey ahead. Embracing a robust Reformed vision of theology is clearly a very live option for some. Others play for time by joining the fashionable Emergent Movement, trusting that in time something will emerge that will be relevant to a new generation of seekers (they retain the afterglow of their initial evangelistic fervor).

Turning to the Future

The solution to this strikes me as simple. What theology gave, she should now take back. Thus she needs to reclaim scripture. However, in reclaiming scripture she needs to reclaim an older and much better vision both of scripture and of her work. I can only begin to map out what is at stake here, but we can begin from Gabler himself. I shall explore Gabler's faint hints when I examine this whole matter in my next lecture. In that lecture I want to look at the work of two leading evangelical biblical scholars, Richard Bauckham and N. T. Wright, who have tried to find a better way into the future.

2. Evangelicals and the Authority of Scripture

> Christianity is not the sacrifice we make, but the sacrifice we trust; not the victory we win, but the victory we inherit. That is the evangelical principle. We do not see the Answerer; we trust the Answerer, and measure by Him. We do not gain the victory; we are united with the Victor. Faith is not simply contact but communion. We do not simply refer our souls to Christ, we commit them. And to commit our souls to Christ is to confess the Godhead of Christ. It would be idolatry to commit our eternal soul to one who differed from us but in degree. Christ crucified and risen is the final, eternal answer to the riddle of life.

P. T. Forsyth. [34]

Getting the Right Epistemology

In my last lecture I proposed that the rise of biblical theology was a pivotal development within Western Christian theology. It did not arise merely because we wanted a proper reading of scripture; it arose because Christian systematic theology had gotten itself into a mess after the Reformation and had therefore invented biblical theology to get out of that

---

[34] Forsyth, *Justification of God*, 230.

mess. Systematic theologians had come to develop a very particular epistemology of theology as a way of resolving first-order disagreement. Their hope was that if they could only deploy the right method of justification for beliefs then they could settle their disputes; disputes that had reached the point of death for the protagonists. The favored epistemology was simple: turn to scripture as the crucial if not sole warrant for theology and then we will find the answers we need. Hence the creation of biblical theology as the foundation of all theology was a kind of accident waiting to happen in the bosom of Western Christian theology.

Modern evangelical theology is one of the most important heirs to this strategy for resolving theological disputes. While the evangelical movement across its history is incredibly diverse, I have in mind initially the standard brand that one meets in the contemporary academy and that was really a reworking of Fundamentalism. The quest for a viable account of the authority of scripture is a perennial one among such evangelicals. In this, of course, they are not alone. The topic continues to rumble around all over the theological landscape like a bad migraine. No matter how much medicine we take the topic keeps coming back to haunt us.

By the *authority of scripture* I mean a theory of scripture that focuses on scripture as a solution to problems in epistemology. It is important that we be clear about what we mean here. Not every problem we face is an epistemological problem. Put differently, epistemology arises at some distance down the line from the making of this or that assertion. Consider a simple progression of statements. First, I make the assertion that God is Triune. I simply make a truth claim. Second, I then give the reason for this claim; that this assertion, or doctrine, is either present in or can be derived from scripture. So I seek to ground my first assertion in some way in scripture. The citation from scripture constitutes a reason for holding the truth I am asserting. Third, I then provide a theory of scripture that grounds that move. I insist that scripture is best seen as a form of divine revelation. It is at this third level that epistemology arises.[35] At this stage, we are in the business of providing deep justifications or warrants for our truth claims. We are laying

---

[35] The whole field of epistemology is up for grabs at the moment, but there is enough stability to make my point. A comprehensive theory of knowledge needs a theory of truth because truth is integral to knowledge; truth is a necessary condition of knowledge.

claim not just to know, nor just to give reasons for what we claim to know, but we are also showing how we know, or showing that we are entitled to know. More specifically, we are offering the beginnings of an epistemology of theology. So to develop a vision of the authority of scripture is to commit ourselves in a robust manner to an epistemology of theology; it is to answer third-level queries about justification and warrant; it is to develop an epistemic theory of scripture.

The Status of Epistemology

Now that we have a relatively clear picture of what an epistemic vision of scripture is and the kind of discussion it precipitates, we are in a position to pose the question that seldom, if ever, gets asked. What is the place of this kind of theory in the life of faith, in the church, and in theology itself? What is the status of a theory of knowledge or of truth?

For evangelicals who bet the store on the authority of scripture, it is obvious that this matter is of absolutely critical significance. Failing to make the grade in this arena is thought to be a life or death phenomenon. It would be tedious to set out to prove this in any extended fashion. The evidence in terms of repeated avowals, boundary maintenance, homiletical warnings, faculty firings, intellectual suspicion, confessions of faith, and the like, lies all around us. Sometimes the issue is pressed in terms of proper foundations for theology. Without proper grounding in the authority of scripture, it is thought that everything will collapse; truth, the gospel, morality, salvation, missions, holiness, orthodox Christianity, and the unity of the church are all at stake. Without a proper criterion of truth in theology it is imagined that we will all drown in a raging sea of relativism, nihilism, subjectivism, cultural accommodation, hermeneutical narcissism, nihilism and a whole host of other disasters. Evangelicals who venture forth, say, into postmodernity, are at particular risk, for postmodernity is generally taken to mean the end of foundationalism in theology; and the end of foundationalism means the end of the authority of scripture as commonly understood in its epistemic instantiations. Moreover, some vision of the authority of scripture has been taken to be constitutive of Evangelicalism, so, at the very least, abandoning the authority of scripture would seem to mean the end of Evangelicalism. The stakes are indeed high.

There is, however, historically speaking, another and equally important side to Evangelicalism in its approach to scripture. I have in mind the valiant efforts on the part of evangelicals to keep alive the canon of scripture as a pivotal means of grace within the church. In this instance the great heroes and heroines are not to be found in the intellectual centers of theology but in the evangelical underworld of bible study groups, movements, fellowships, associations, societies, revival meetings, and the like. The treasures of the tradition in this case are found in the spiritual materials and practices of the tradition, that is, in preaching, scriptural commentaries, pious calendars, hymnody, gospel songs, love feasts, class meetings, covenant groups, prayer meetings, annual revivals, and annual conferences. They are to be located in pietism, Methodism, the Society of Quakers, revivalism, the Salvation Army, Pentecostalism, and the modern Charismatic movement. The heroes of the tradition are Philipp Spener (1635-1705) and August Francke (1663-1727), John Wesley (1703-1791) and George Whitefield (1714-1770), Charles Finney (1792-1875) and D. L. Moody (1837-1899), William Booth (1829-1912) and Catherine Booth (1829-1890).

It is worth stopping for a moment and insisting on two related points before we move on. First, the version of Evangelicalism of which I speak is every bit as legitimate a version of this noble tradition as its more recent cousin which broke from Fundamentalism. As a noisy and pervasive version of Evangelicalism it is rightly associated with the Awakenings of the eighteenth and nineteenth centuries. It is all too often seen as weak-minded, emotional, and anti-intellectual. The primary emphases fall on new birth and sanctification. To be sure, these bring with them their own liabilities and potential vices. However, they also foster their own inimitable intellectual challenges that result in their own unique contribution to the life of the mind. In some instances, contrary to the standard stereotype, the results are remarkable.[36]

Second, one of the deep blind spots in the history of theology, and even in Christianity in the West, is the scant attention paid to Methodism and its impact across space and

---

[36] I have charted elsewhere the surprising moves in epistemology that show up, for example, in the work of John Wesley. See William J. Abraham, *Aldersgate and Athens: John Wesley and the Foundations of Christian Belief* (Waco, Tex: Baylor University Press, 2010).

time. Truth be told, Methodism has not only spawned its own range of dogmatic theology well into the nineteenth century; it has also given birth to some of the most vibrant forms of contemporary Christianity across the Global South. This extremely important shift in demographics is beginning to get attention even in secular circles. However, the reorientation that is so sorely needed in historical and theological studies remains a challenge that is little recognized, much less addressed.

If I am broadly right about the presence of an alternative vision of scripture in Evangelicalism then one obvious way ahead is surely to develop a thoroughly soteriological conception of scripture. This would surely fit with one element in J. P. Gabler's vision, which we discussed last time. The different vision of scripture that Gabler hints at comes out in two ways. It emerges explicitly in the recurring concern with salvation that runs through his address. Here is one of his hints. Speaking of exegeting the apostles, he confidently notes: "...it may finally be established whether all the opinions of the Apostles, of every type and sort altogether, are *truly divine*, or rather whether some of them *which have no bearing on salvation*, were left to their own ingenuity."[37] The key phrase here is "which have no bearing on salvation," a feature of the text that Gabler identifies with the "truly divine." This hint surely dovetails with the other concern that crops up, namely, the fact that people turn to scripture as a sanctuary where they can get a solid understanding of divine matters, and where they might obtain a firm and certain hope of salvation. They do not turn to scripture just because it may be great literature, or because it helps sort through their questions about ancient Near Eastern antiquities; they turn to scripture in order to wise up once they become concerned about salvation.

We can surely see here a rival vision of the function of scripture, namely, scripture simply as a place where folk can find deliverance and salvation. What is at work here is a robustly soteriological conception of scripture as opposed to an epistemological account. On this analysis scripture functions as a complex means of grace to awaken us to our spiritual diseases and to draw us to living faith in God.

[37] Sandys-Wunsch and Eldredge, "J. P. Gabler and the Distinction between Biblical and Dogmatic Theology," 143, emphasis mine.

It is precisely this soteriological vision of scripture that needs to be retrieved and put to work in the present. It needs also to be extended to become the heart and soul of theology itself; for once we abandon the epistemological conception of scripture we also undermine the standard vision of theology that we have inherited in the West and that still haunts the landscape.

The challenge before us now is obvious. Can contemporary evangelicals make this transition cleanly and unequivocally?

Happily some evangelicals are trying to make it. Let me examine in some detail two examples: Richard Bauckham and N. T. Wright. Both are distinguished New Testament scholars. Both of them set enormous store by the concept of narrative, a move that is very attractive across the board in many contemporary theologies of scripture.[38] Moreover, both of them in their work reflect a focus on the inductive study of scripture, that is, an emphasis on scripture as it actually is, rather than scripture as read from within a

---

[38] The notion of narrative is exploited skillfully in the service of feminist theology in Sarah Heaner Lancaster, *Women and the Authority of Scripture: A Narrative Approach* (Harrisburg, Pa: Trinity Press International, 2002).

particular theory of scripture enshrined in, say, a theory of divine inspiration. In this shift to the inductive they represent perhaps a British tendency that shows up in the nineteenth century in the work of William Sanday and in the twentieth century in the work of James Barr and David Brown.

The Work of Richard Bauckham

A neat way into Bauckham's analysis is by making a distinction between extrinsic and intrinsic authority. In the case of extrinsic authority you rely on someone outside of you, say, a doctor or a friend. In the case of intrinsic authority, you see for yourself what is the case. "The statement convinces you, so that you accept it as true and do what it requires of you."[39] The authority of the Bible is a combination of these elements. Initially Christians take it on trust. They believe scripture because "what it says should be believed because God has the authority to say it."[40] However, as they grow in the faith, the scriptures are authenticated in their own experience, what it says makes more and more

[39] Richard Bauckham, *Scripture and Authority Today* (Cambridge: Grove Books, 1999), 3.
[40] Ibid., 4.

sense to them existentially, intellectually, imaginatively.

As Bauckham sees the current scene both modernists and postmodernists really reject the whole idea of authority. Modernists do so because, like Kant, they reject extrinsic authority. They rely on a narrow conception of reason, of what "can be demonstrated empirically from first principles in a way that is universally accessible."[41] While this move rightly develops a necessary critique of authoritarianism, it wrongly posits a false antithesis between autonomy and freedom. Postmodernists turn this critique back on modernists by insisting that modernists are authoritarian in that they impose a very particular tradition of thought on everybody else under the guise of universality. What was offered as freedom and rationality was really a form of domination, an exercise in power. Against this postmodernists insist that all truth is somebody's truth and that we must be free to believe our own personal truth. Hence postmodernists celebrate particularity and diversity, unmasking all beliefs as instruments in the struggle of diverse interest groups for power. In addition they rapidly develop a

[41] Ibid., 6.

political agenda to include those marginalized and suppressed groups that have been ignored by the modern tradition. What is on offer then is a more radical version of freedom and liberation than that generally offered by the Enlightenment. In some instances they reject the very authority of science itself (even medical science) and are quick to embrace a ready espousal of pick-and-mix choice in worldview. Clearly, the authority of scripture fares badly in this alien environment. "To the authority of the Bible's claim to truth which is valid for all people postmodernism is probably even less hospitable than modernism."[42]

Bauckham's initial constructive response to this situation is to offer an account of Bible as story. Indeed story is the fundamental horizon within which to view all of scripture.

> The category of story includes not only biblical narratives—the many smaller narratives, many of them relatively self-contained, but canonically placed within the Bible's total story—but also prophecy and apostolic teaching insofar as these illuminate the meaning of the story and point its direction towards its

[42] Ibid., 9.

still future completion. The total biblical story is also the context within which other biblical genres—law, wisdom, psalms, ethical instruction, parables, and so on—are canonically placed.[43]

More to the point, narrative in the form of metanarrative is the key to the authority of scripture. The authority of scripture is the authority of story.

> To accept the authority of this story is to enter it and to inhabit it. It is to live in the world as the world is portrayed in this story. It is to let this story define our identity and our relationship to God and to others. It is to read the narratives of our own lives and of the societies in which we live as narratives that take their meaning from this metanarrative that overreaches them all. To accept this metanarrative as the one within which we live is to see the world differently and to live within it differently from the way we would if we inhabited another metanarrative or framework of universal meaning.[44]

[43] Ibid., 10.
[44] Ibid.

Even more to the point, to accept this metanarrative as authoritative "is to privilege it above all other stories."[45] Stepping inside the story supplied by scripture, we accept its plot as our own; we accept this story as the ultimate horizon for all other stories. Within this story we then play our part in writing the current chapter of the story. We align ourselves with God's purposes, living in a way that anticipates their achievement in a final conclusion that still lies ahead for the cosmos. It is this story, rather than, say the Marxist story of violent revolution; or the Enlightenment story of the march of reason; or Nietzsche's story of self-creation captured in his images of the camel, the lion, and the child; that Christians inhabit.

Some such story is inescapable for human beings. Thus Lyotard in his famous incredulity towards all metanarratives was mistaken. Even the postmodernist has a metanarrative.

> The modernist mastered the world through science and technology; the postmodernist constructs it textually. Retreating into a purely linguistic world of arbitrary signs, the postmodernist

[45] Ibid., 11.

gains freedom from all authority, but leaves the modernist free to continue subjecting the extralinguistic world to abuse.[46]

The attraction of the Bible's story is that it gives us access to true freedom. The biblical metanarrative happily provides a liberating alternative.

This metanarrative, by placing the future in God's hands, liberates us from the need for mastery or control, restoring to us a properly human way of living in relationship with the rest of reality, neither subjecting it to our will nor constructing it at will. This depends on recognizing the kind of authority the metanarrative attributes to God as the authority of grace.[47]

We have traveled a long way from the idea of intrinsic and extrinsic authority. These are hopelessly thin epistemic notions as they stand. By this point we have pretty much abandoned them altogether, and with them we have abandoned the world of epistemology. We are now in the world of first-order

[46] Ibid., 13.
[47] Ibid.

assertion, of spiritual formation, and of grace. To be sure, we also have the standard global (not to say totalizing and reductionistic) accounts of cultural change in the West over the last three centuries. So we also have a slice of cultural history. However, the crucial observation to be made is simple. None of this material is recognizably epistemological; it is mostly straight assertion of the story of scripture together with comments on how to live into its plot as it moves into the future. This dovetails with the rest of Bauckham's proposals. Thus the authority of grace is spelled out in terms of a theological anthropology in which the assertion of autonomy against domination is replaced by the assertion of grace and free response. We can also state this move in terms of divine action. God covenants with us in Israel and in Christ and enables us to respond in gratitude and trust. In time the authority of God is seen as the natural home of free human obedience and love in which we accept for ourselves, as friends of Jesus, the commandments given to us. We have the final identity of human freedom and divine authority.

Where do these fascinating proposals lead us in ethics and doctrine? The answer is: not very far. On ethics we are given a direction with diversity. "In discerning the direction in the diversity we come to a richer understanding of an issue and its outworking in the diversity of human life than a single straightforward pronouncement could afford us."[48] In doctrine we are given a skeleton doctrine of the Trinity. The story is Trinitarian in form. "A doctrine of the Trinity represents what we need to say about God in God's self for the biblical story of God to be a true story. It follows from taking the story seriously as authoritative metanarrative."[49] In both these cases we are then authorized to do and to say things we could never say or do on our own, most especially to speak of God.

Of course, we have to read and listen to the text of scripture in the right way. We are forbidden to go the way of control, that is, with the aim of ferreting out "the meaning that the first readers could be expected to find in the text."[50] We are equally forbidden to read the text in a way that is subject to our authority as we create our own meaning. Rather, meaning happens in the interaction between text and readers, with each having the freedom to address each other. While such reading is done in community, we must be

[48] Ibid., 18.
[49] Ibid.
[50] Ibid., 20.

careful to leave room for the voices of the individual or marginal group.

The Work of N.T. Wright

It is clear that N.T. Wright is playing off a very similar wicket to that of Richard Bauckham in his characteristically lively work on biblical authority.[51] Thus he insists the debate about the authority of scripture is really about the authority of God, that the crucial category to deploy is that of narrative and that the narrative of scripture is best seen as a play with five acts.[52] He also supplies an evaluative account of modern and postmodern culture (placing it in the narrative of the use of scripture across the whole history of the church); he insists on paying careful attention to genre and to the actual bible we use in the church; and he gives various constructive suggestions on how to read scripture properly. Materially Wright, following the work of George Caird, has sought to place the

[51] See N. T. Wright, "How Can The Bible Be Authoritative?" originally published in *Vox Evangelica*, 21, 7-32 (1991) and *Scripture and the Authority of God* (London: SPCK, 2005).
[52] The five acts as developed in *The New Testament and the People of God* (London: SPCK, 1992) are: creation, "fall", Israel, Jesus, and the church.

authority of scripture within the field of eschatology, that is, within a dense account of the arrival of God's kingdom here and in the future. It is this focus on eschatology, developed with extraordinary erudition, exegetical detail, homiletical brilliance, and intellectual passion, that sets his work apart in the current scene. What it also does is take the whole discussion out of the field of epistemology, even though the echoes of the old context keep popping back up from time to time. Bits and pieces of the language of epistemology remain but they are idling.

The crux of my point is this: for Wright scripture is no longer a norm or criterion of truth, it is fundamentally a means of grace used by the Holy Spirit to establish people in the kingdom of God and equip them for appropriate response and service. "One might even say, in one (admittedly limited) sense, that there is no biblical doctrine of the authority of the Bible. For the most part the Bible itself is much more concerned with doing a whole range of other things rather than talking about itself."[53] What are these other things? Let me roll out a catalogue of what the Bible does, as Wright sees it.

---

[53] Wright, "How Can The Bible Be Authoritative?", 3.

Virtually all of them have to do with what I will call God's causal action or efficacy. Through the scriptures God operates "to liberate human beings, to judge and condemn evil and sin in the world in order to set people free to be fully human."[54] God gave us a play in various acts, authorizing the church to work through the fifth act for itself. The Bible "is not merely a divinely given commentary on the way salvation works (or whatever); the Bible is part of the means by which he [God] puts his purposes of judgment and salvation to work."[55] Standing first in the councils of the creator God, the church is then to stand in the councils of human agents. How so? "By soaking ourselves in scripture, in the power and strength and leading of the Holy Spirit, in order that we may then then speak freshly and with authority to the world of this same creator God."[56] "Through scripture, God is [was] equipping his people to serve his purposes."[57]

> The emergence of a 'canon' of scripture…was at its heart an attempt to

[54] Ibid., 8.
[55] Ibid., 11.
[56] Ibid., 12.
[57] Wright, *Scripture and the Authority of God*, 27.

track the way in which *these* books had become formative for the life of God's people, to honor the fact that God had somehow given them to his people, and to remind Israel to honor them and attend to them appropriately. And in and through it all we find the elusive but powerful idea of God's "word", not as a synonym for the written scriptures, but as a strange personal presence, creating, judging, healing, recreating.[58]

The apostolic writings, like the "word" which they now wrote down, were not simply *about* the coming of God's Kingdom into all the world; they were, and were designed to be, part of the *means whereby they happened*, and whereby those through whom it happened could themselves be transformed into Christ's likeness.[59]

When we ponder these remarks cumulatively it is clear, to use Wright's own language as applied to scripture in the Enlightenment, that "the phrase 'authority of scripture' has been deconstructed to vanishing

[58] Ibid., 28. Emphasis as in the original.
[59] Ibid., 38.

point."[60] We have shifted from the language of norm, criterion, justification, knowledge, and the like to the language of kingdom, salvation, liberation, equipping, formation, and the like. We have shifted from epistemology to soteriology.

Yet Wright regresses from time to time. When one expects him to applaud John Webster's remarkable relocation of the doctrine of scripture to the arena of pneumatology and sanctification, he complains that Webster does not focus on what the text actually says.

> ...one would never have known from reading this book, anything at all about what the Bible contains...since his thesis is that scripture is the central source for all Christian thinking, it might have been appropriate (and not beyond the wit of such a fine scholar) to base his contention, too, on scripture itself.[61]

Webster does indeed have a problem on his hands. Here is this splendid Reformed

---

[60] Ibid., 64.
[61] Ibid., 10. J. B. Webster's book *Holy Scripture A Dogmatic Sketch* (Cambridge: Cambridge University Press, 2003) is one of the finest to occur of late in the debate about scripture.

theologian, one of the jewels of English-speaking theology at the moment, offering a vision of scripture that presupposes rather than establishes the doctrine of the Trinity. Wright, however, has exactly the same problem. As noted above he tells us, albeit guardedly, that there is no biblical doctrine of the authority of scripture.[62] He then reverses himself: "...within the second half of this lecture, I want to suggest that scripture's own view of authority focuses on the authority of God himself."[63] Wright has other very serious problems too. An acute difficulty is that Wright dismisses the very skills that are needed at this point, namely, the kind of conceptual work that is done within analytical philosophy. He is clearly living in the world that existed prior to the revolutionary developments in epistemology that have arisen since the seventies. The indispensable text on the concept of authority is, of course, Richard T. De George, *The Nature and Limits of Authority* (Lawrence: The University Press of Kansas, 1985). Yet Wright totally ignores

---

[62] Wright also rightly refuses to be intimidated by those who think that they can appeal to the theology of Jesus to trap him, as if Jesus was a great epistemologist of theology. See his *Scripture and the Authority of God*, chapter 5.

[63] Wright, "How Can The Bible Be Authoritative?", 6.

this kind of work. An even more acute problem is the fact that it is hard to see how the canon can provide an account of its own nature. It is the church that creates and identifies the canon; and it is theologians of the church who provide theories of its nature and purpose. The old rhetoric of a biblical view of authority has outlived its usefulness. It is time to abandon it once and for all and move forward without it.

It is small wonder that, while Wright's biblical scholarship is surely one of the great treasures of contemporary Evangelicalism, his evangelical credentials have been called into question in some quarters. He is clearly wobbling between an epistemic and soteriological conception of scripture. The material direction, however, is clear. His primary categories are theological and soteriological rather than epistemological. On the score of evangelical identity, Wright takes no prisoners. He deftly confounds his critics in all sorts of ways, not least by noting how often evangelical visions of scripture end up captive to the very human traditions that they formally eschew and excoriate. They prevent scripture from being itself and from the host of things it actually does in the church and in the life of faith.

The wider point that needs to be made at this stage, however, is historical and conceptual. Many evangelicals have stood exactly where Wright stands. Their primary vision in scripture, revealed in practice and theory, has been soteriological. They have looked to scripture to make us wise unto salvation, to teach and transmit all things necessary to salvation, to be the means whereby sinners are awakened to and then led into radical faith in Jesus Christ as Savior and Lord. Donald Dayton has made the case for this with telling specificity and candor.[64] Dayton has pursued this topic as part of a wider inquiry into the historiography of Evangelicalism. Dayton wants to take us into his own vision of liberation theology via Pietism and Pentecostalism. I prefer a very different alternative, one that would, I think, actually be more congenial to Bauckham and Wright because of its ecclesiological leanings and depth. However, I am more than glad to acknowledge my Pietist underwear and pedigree, and I have no interest in a vision of the gospel that stays clear of politics and the

---

[64] Donald Dayton, "The Pietist Theological Critique of Biblical Inerrancy," in Vincent Bacote, Laura C. Miguélez, and Dennis L. Okholm, eds., *Evangelicals & Scripture* (Downers Grove, Ill: Intervarsity Press, 2004), 76-89.

public square. However, on the bigger picture (the importance of a soteriological vision of scripture) I think that Dayton is exactly right. So I shall not repeat his case here. What I want to do instead is to repeat a wider suggestion and answer an obvious objection.

On not Fudging on the Need for Radical Reorientation

Let me approach my suggestion by way of an observation. Many evangelicals are wary of the position of Bauckham and Wright because it is theologically thin not *de facto* but *de jure*, not contingently but normatively. In this I think they are correct. Evangelicals rightly worry that Christian theology will be at the mercy of that fifth act, the church. *De facto*, of course, Bauckham and Wright will supply a rich and robust theism. The question is whether they are entitled to it *de jure*. However, evangelicals who focus on the epistemic vision of scripture run exactly the same gauntlet. Because they continue to press the issue of the authority of scripture, because the first move is always epistemological and methodological, they end up destabilizing the faith. We have to wait until the exegetes finish their work, until the hermeneutical experts get it right about interpretation, until the philosophers underwrite the theory of divine revelation below the surface, and until the theologians once again give the faith of the church a clean bill of health, before we can really trust the faith of the church. They are in exactly the same boat as Bauckham and Wright and their fifth act, that is, with respect to the church.[65]

Evangelicals should also worry about the ready deployment of the idea of story. They should worry about the inflated use of story not simply because it is utterly implausible to try and shoe-horn all of scripture into this model; nor because narrative is a wax nose that can be manipulated at will to fit what one wants. Above all they should worry because the idea of story cannot secure the great faith of the church as a living, active, constitutive component of salvation.

In actual fact we owe the great narrative of creation and redemption not to scripture but to Irenaeus and the other early theologians of the tradition who lodged scripture inside the rule of faith (and ultimately the canonical Creed of the Church developed at Nicaea and Constantinople) that was handed over in

---

[65] I leave aside the long-lasting problem of unity that results from unending takes on the scriptures that has bedeviled Protestantism. Wright is very aware of this.

baptism and catechesis and that was crucial in fending off the rival Gnostic narratives to which they subjected the developing canon of scripture in regards to both content and boundaries. The best way to capture the deep theology of the church is to revisit the idea of canon as a list, to exploit the purpose of canon as a means of grace, and then to come to terms with the full canonical heritage of the church that the Holy Spirit has given us. I have argued that it is in exactly this direction that evangelicals who want to preserve the best treasures of Evangelicalism should go.[66] It is the insisting on the primacy of an epistemic conception of scripture and canon that prevents the ready embrace of the Trinitarian faith of the church as an indispensable means of grace. It is a soteriological conception of scripture that creates the opening for deep reliance on the creed as a canonical means of grace. Wobbling between the two simply leaves neither side satisfied. We need to make a clean break with the epistemological tradition

[66] See "Canonical Theism and Evangelicalism," in *Canonical Theism: A Proposal for Theology and the Church*, edited by William J. Abraham, Jason E. Vickers, and Natalie B. Van Kirk (Grand Rapids, Mich: William B. Eerdmans, 2008).

on scripture and make the full transition into a soteriological vision.

In casting the debate about scripture as a debate about authority, we ignore this critical distinction. Many evangelicals reach first and last for a vision of scripture that is cast in epistemological categories. They want a robust epistemology of theology, a laudable enterprise; but in the process they suffer losses both in epistemology and soteriology. In epistemology they cook the books to fit their initial position, or they systematically ignore the radical diversity of options available to the robust theist in contemporary epistemology. In soteriology they impoverish their ministries as they become captive to the latest fads in epistemology. There is a whole industry geared to exploiting cultural changes decked out as epistemological revolutions. Bauckham and Wright have seen all this and much more. Hence they reach for a soteriological vision of scripture. Yet they are still stuck with the old category of authority and fail to follow through on their best insights.

Of course, the astute among us, like the wonderfully erudite Kevin Vanhoozer, immediately insist we can have our cake and eat it. We can have scripture both as a norm and as a means of grace. Jesus brings us both grace and truth. The apostolic witness is both a norm and a means of grace. The renewal of the mind is an aspect of one's sanctification.[67] So surely I have mistakenly opted for a sharp either/or when we can all have an irenic both/and. It is that sharp either/or that I want to keep firmly in place for the sake of both epistemology and the gospel. Vanhoozer is simply mistaken. In claiming that Jesus brings us grace and truth he confuses bringing truth with bringing an epistemology. To have truth is not to have an epistemology. The same applies to the apostolic witness that Vanhoozer has surreptitiously substituted for the canon of scripture. To have the apostolic witness is not to have an epistemology. To see the renewal of one's mind as integral to sanctification is not even the first step in epistemology. For that we need a lot more; we need serious attention to the concept of truth and to other pivotal concepts like intellectual virtue, epistemic practices, rationality, justification, and of course knowledge itself. Nowhere does either Jesus or the apostolic witness or the precious scriptures or appeal to the renewal of our minds give us an

---

[67] Kevin J. Vanhoozer, *The Drama of Doctrine: A Canonical-Linguistic Approach to Christian Theology* (Louisville: Westminster John Knox Press, 2005), 144-45.

epistemology; it is a bogus form of theological and spiritual inflation to claim that this is the case.

In his footnotes Vanhoozer goes on to make two interesting comments. In one he says that in my own work I am suffering from a confusion of categories when I somehow claim that it is one thing to appeal to scripture as an authority and quite another to appeal to scripture as a solution to epistemological questions. He cites page three of the relevant text but no such confusion can be located there. In another footnote he says: "Abraham's concern to rescue Scripture from epistemology parallels Harnack's concern to rescue the gospel from metaphysics."[68] Even though it is nice to find myself in the company of Harnack, this is a cryptic remark devoid of explanatory content. At worst it is an effort at guilt by association; at best it a misleading reading of my concerns. The issue is not the gospel and metaphysics but scripture and epistemology. Whatever the formal similarities Vanhoozer perceives here, the crucial issue is the material claims we advance; these are not resolved by dragging in

---

[68] Ibid., footnote 98, 145

Harnack as some kind of placeholder for an argument.

To be sure, both scripture (and the apostolic witness within it) and Jesus give us all sorts of epistemic insights and proto-theory. Such insights need to be mined for all they are worth in working through a full epistemology of theology. Indeed I would go further: we need a robust, industrial strength vision of divine revelation centering on the incarnation of the Son of God as the very nerve center of knowledge of God.[69] But these are strictly midrash in the church. They go way beyond the plethora of epistemological insights that scripture has to offer. Our great God and Savior, Jesus Christ, readily gives us grace and truth in the absence of such grand developments. It is a matter of urgency for Evangelicalism and for Protestantism more generally to remember this and to put its house in good working order. Shifting to a soteriological vision of scripture is one crucial step, but not the only step, to achieve this end. Evangelicals need a death and resurrection not bland platitudes about a both/and at this point in our history.

---

[69] I have sought to spell out the backbone of what this means in my *Crossing the Threshold of Divine Revelation* (Grand Rapids, Mich: William B. Eerdmans Pub, 2006).

In my final lecture I shall try and pull all this together and drive it home thoroughly and forcefully.

3. Onwards and Upwards

We are not here like hunters who care everything for the chase and nothing for the quarry. The quest does promise conquest. The riddle of the painful earth has its final answer. The Christian message is that the answer is there, and is the gift of God. It is provided. And it is practical. It is done more than spoken, and done to our hand. We are not asked to waste our labour on the insoluble. At the risk of being called dogmatists the Church, the pulpit, the Gospel are all there to say there is a solution, that it is given us rather than won by us, and already done and not merely shown. If there is no foregone solution, these voices have no right to speak. But they say there is a solution, and they not only say there is, but they are there to bring it, and give it, and stake life on it. As man dogmatises to nature, God dogmatises to man. 'There remaineth a rest for the people of God.'

P.T. Forsyth[70]

Introduction: Resetting the Scene

In my first two lectures I argued two theses. First, systematic theology set up biblical studies as a feeder-discipline because of a vision of its own task as a kind of *scientia* with appropriate foundations; scripture was

[70] Forsyth, *Justification of God*, 220.

conceived precisely in such a way as to supply the foundations. It fell to the genius of Johannes Gabler to articulate the rationale for this experiment with pleasing clarity. This experiment in biblical theology has turned out to be a failure. Second, one way out of his failure is to retrieve a very different vision of scripture, namely to receive scripture soteriologically, as a critical means of grace. This gets us on the right track, even though making the relevant change in orientation is far from easy, as we were able to observe in the work of Richard Bauckham and N. T. Wright. Bauckham and Wright are trying valiantly to meet a whole new crisis for evangelical theology, a crisis as deep and difficult as was faced when Gabler did his work.

However, much more is needed than a shift of conceptual gears. We need to go way beyond this conceptual shift. Not only do we need to rethink the meaning of the concept of canon, we need to revisit what constituted its referent, and then to think through afresh what we should be doing in systematic theology. Ancillary to this we need to develop a new sub-discipline in theology and philosophy, namely, the epistemology of theology in order to address the issues that first generated the vision of scripture as a criterion of truth in theology.

Fixing the Epistemology

We can, of course, think of other options. In broad terms, I want to suggest four substantial responses to the crisis I have identified.

First, we can simply give up scripture as the foundation of theology and find other foundations for theology in reason, experience, tradition, or whatever, and start all over again in theology. I have argued elsewhere that, if we keep this option in mind, modern theology can profitably be read as a wild goose chase to find the right foundations for theology; moreover, that goose chase should be called off once and for all.[71]

Second, we can give up the search for foundations, find some other way to think of the epistemology of theology, and then start again from scratch. It is clear that this option is flourishing in biblical studies, in philosophy, and in theology, so we can expect to hear more from those who favor this way forward.

[71] This is the central thesis of the latter part of my *Canon and Criterion in Christian Theology: From the Fathers to Feminism* (Oxford: Clarendon Press, 1998).

Third, we can go back in and try to rework our vision of scripture as norm and then go back to work all over again in theology. No doubt this will mean a new vision of biblical studies where the theologians will have to lend significant help, but so be it, it will be said. Perhaps theologians should simply take to doing biblical studies themselves, acquiring whatever skills they need to get the job done. It is this, surely, or something akin to this, that is fuelling the new commentary series by Brazos Press. The lead volume is the remarkable commentary on Acts by Jaroslav Pelikan, *Acts* (Grand Rapids, Mich: Brazos Press, 2005). Other commentary series, like the *Two Horizons* series from Eerdmans, may also fit this agenda. It is clear that we have a similar type of move in Kevin J. Vanhoozer, ed., *Dictionary for Theological Interpretation of the Bible* (Grand Rapids, MI: Baker Academic, 2005).[72]

Fourth, another option is to shore up the problem of divergent interpretations of scripture by the formal adoption of a vision of

---

[72] Interestingly this is not the thinking behind the new series of theological commentaries forthcoming from Westminster John Knox press where the commentators will be given much greater latitude in their theological conception of scripture.

papal infallibility, that is, by seeking out an epistemic office and mechanism that, under the tutelage of tradition and the sense of the faithful, clearly tells us what scripture really teaches on critical matters of faith and morals. It is clear from the wonderful flowering of scripture scholarship in recent Catholicism that this option has already borne much fruit. Rome offers a very sophisticated interaction between historical investigation and the teaching *magisterium* of the church that is more than enough to keep the most skilled and talented scholar hard at work for a lifetime. Contrary to first impressions, nineteenth and twentieth century Roman Catholicism has the ironic effect of saving the central tenets of conservative Protestant doctrines of scripture. This development may help partially explain the turn to Rome on the part of a network of younger Protestant theologians in the last decade or so.

The interesting feature of all these options is the way that they privilege epistemology as the way forward. All of them depend on getting the epistemology straight, even if the epistemology is a kind of anti-epistemology, as happens in the case of the second, postmodernist option. It is precisely because of this privileging of epistemology that I refuse all of these options. Having failed with the invention of biblical studies, it is now hoped that epistemology will deliver the goods. Having been hostage to the history department, theologians now sell themselves into captivity to philosophy. Operating as a philosopher I find this solution almost comical.

The correct insight here, of course, is that we need more and not less work in the epistemology of theology. Too much of the theology currently on offer involves half-hearted, half-baked epistemology. This is especially otiose when we are in the midst of a golden period for philosophy of religion, as represented by Basil Mitchell, Richard Swinburne, Alvin Plantinga, William Alston, Nicholas Wolterstorff, Eleonore Stump, and a host of others. We also live in a golden period of epistemology, much of it developed by robust theists.[73] So it would be silly to disparage work in epistemology just at the time when it has opened up all sorts of insights for theology.[74] We need more and much better work in the epistemology of

[73] I speak here in this work only of the Anglo-American analytical tradition, but we should not limit ourselves to this strain; we need all hands on deck.

[74] For my own formal contribution to the discussion see *Crossing the Threshold of Divine Revelation.*

theology not less. The mistake is to think that epistemological considerations must be resolved first before we can begin the real work of theology. We should not bet the life of the church on the success of this or that epistemology of theology. We have lost that bet too many times to want to try it again. Let me dwell on this bet for a moment.

Losing Bets on Epistemology

How can an epistemological bet be lost? I suggest there are two ways, one material and one formal.

In the case of a material challenge the epistemology on offer cannot cope with first-order claims that call into question the legitimacy of the epistemology. One can think of various cases that have cropped up in general epistemology. Suppose I am a utilitarian and I am convinced that the criterion of adequacy for moral claims is that the actions identified lead to the greatest happiness to the greatest number of people. I then think of someone roasting babies alive at three o'clock in the morning for fun. It so happens that in the circumstances envisaged this action actually leads to the greatest happiness to the greatest number of people involved. However, my stand on the correctness of this particular material claim strikes me as having more weight than my initial epistemology. It simply undermines my epistemology of morality as represented by utilitarianism.

Alternatively, suppose I am a rationalist and will only accept as true those propositions that are intuitively certain. I then come to believe that common sense claims of perception are true. I come to think that I really do know that there is a tree in the yard, even though I may be deceived by my senses, by an evil demon, or by a mad scientist who has reduced me to a brain in a vat. In this instance the rationalism collapses. Something like this happened to Thomas Reid and G. E. Moore. Reid and Moore simply came to privilege particular beliefs, say, about personal agents and ordinary household objects over the epistemologies they inherited. This is often missed, as it was by Kant in the case of Reid, when it is thought that Reid and Moore are simply pitting common sense against this or that philosophy. What is at issue is that Reid and Moore were more convinced by the truth of particular material claims than about received epistemological doctrines and were prepared to turn them against epistemological theories that denied them. The radical revolution in epistemology they represent was a matter of epistemological insight not dogmatic assertion.

Many of our problems with claims about the authority of scripture mirror this sort of difficulty. There are hosts of ways in which material claims cause deep trouble and anxiety. People find contradictions within scripture. They find an error in the history. They come to think that scripture makes scientific claims that turn out to be false. They become convinced that scripture endorses horrendous human behavior. They come to believe that the vision of God in scripture undermines human flourishing. They come to believe that women should not be subordinate to men. They embrace a historical reading of the production of the canon that does not fit with what is required by their appeal to scripture. They notice that some texts in scripture were fixed to accommodate the theology of the Church. In these cases we do not initially make epistemological claims; epistemological claims arise as knock-on effects. The received epistemology collapses because it is incompatible with some first order claim that turns out to be epistemically more privileged than the epistemology of theology as expressed in the theory of scripture will allow.

To be sure, many people weather the storms. They find any and every way to remove the cognitive dissonance. They take time out spiritually and settle the issue once and for all, resolving to grit their theological teeth and live with the difficulties as mysteries that they will never be able to settle. They can offer various rebuttals to the material claims that clash with a robust epistemic reading of scripture. They can even adopt the expedient of reworking any untoward interpretation of scripture by shifting from a more literal to a more figurative reading of the text. Thus there is no reason why the most radical Bultmanian cannot hold to the highest view of the authority of scripture and equally be committed to a historical skepticism. The dissonance dissolves by shifting to a reinterpretation of what God has said in scripture that fits with historical skepticism. This is commonly the case in interpretations of the early chapters of Genesis. God can still be construed as the author of scripture; it is the genre that is at stake. There is no reason in the world why God cannot author good myths, including resurrection myths.[75] We can surely

---

[75] Compare a humorous analogy. If God were to author some jokes, we can be sure that those with a good sense of humor would laugh.

see here one reason why evangelicals invest so much time and effort in hermeneutics. They do so not simply because they want to be careful and faithful interpreters of scripture as "authored" by God; they also have to keep at bay interpretations of scripture that will radically undermine the evangelical theology by which they live and pray.

The other way, that is the formal way, for epistemological claims to be undermined is for them to be undermined by other epistemological claims. Thus radical empiricism might be undermined because it lays claim to provide an account of scientific assertions. On further investigation, say, after reading Thomas Kuhn's *The Structure of Scientific Revolutions*,[76] one comes to a much richer account of the justification of scientific claims and forthwith the radical empiricism is undone. Consider another example. Suppose one is a foundationalist, whether radical or moderate. Then suppose one becomes convinced that an element of coherence enters into justification. Perhaps one develops an argument from the place of concepts or language in all descriptions of reality and comes to see that foundationalism must be

[76] Thomas S. Kuhn, *The Structure of Scientific Revolutions* (Chicago: University of Chicago Press, 1962).

false because of this semantic insight. The initial epistemology is undermined by a competing epistemology.

Many of the problems that crop up around the authority of scripture are precipitated by the attraction of alternative epistemological schemas. Thus one comes to place authority in the church, or in reason, or in experience, or in tradition, and there is then severe strain in trying to reconcile these moves with the authority of scripture. To be more precise, suppose one comes to the conviction, as John Wesley did, that experience of the inner witness of the Holy Spirit is a basic bedrock epistemological category like perception.[77] Then one can easily shift into a form of Liberal Protestantism that seeks to base all one's theological proposals on religious experience, and the appeal to scripture can readily become a cipher for an entirely different epistemology. Alternatively, suppose one comes to believe that the poor and the oppressed have privileged access to the truth about God. It can be a short step further along from this to some versions of Liberation

---

[77] I explore this in William J. Abraham, "The Epistemology of Conversion: Is there Something New?", in Kenneth J. Collins and John H. Tyson, *Conversion in the Wesleyan Tradition* (Nashville: Abingdon Press, 2001), 175-194.

81

theology in which one turns exclusively to the experience of the oppressed as the sole ground of theological claims.

As in the case of material problems there are obvious ways of dealing with these formal difficulties. Thus, many recent Liberation theologians remain staunch Protestants by the simply expedient move of making experience of the oppressed not an epistemological issue but a hermeneutical issue.[78] The oppressed then are understood to have privileged access to the best interpretation of scripture. To take another example, the Methodist quadrilateral is a way to try and pull all the relevant norms together by insisting on an appeal to scripture, tradition, reason, and experience. Here one solves the epistemological problems of theology by the simple and naïve expedient of addition. Expressed pejoratively, we have a shotgun wedding in which the church supplies scripture and tradition and philosophy supplies reason and experience. More controversially, the adoption of papal infallibility was one way to bring to an end the great misery of Protestant chaos in the post-Reformation period in the interpretation

[78] This is the strategy one finds in Justo L. González, *Mañana: Christian Theology from a Hispanic Perspective* (Nashville: Abingdon Press, 1990), for example.

of scripture by insisting on a special epistemic mechanism in the magisterium of the church that would secure a correct reading of the scriptures. Roman Catholicism on this view is not the repudiation of *sola scriptura* or the end of Protestantism; it is its ultimate completion. The pope is the last savior of Protestantism.

Why the Revolution Really Matters

The fundamental mistake I am trying to identify right across the board is precisely this exalting of epistemology. We have had enough of this inflationary paranoia, this exaggerated piety, this secularizing treadmill, this captivity to epistemology, this false reading of the very nature of Christianity, this misrepresentation of the history of the faith, and this narrow reading of the evangelical tradition. Indeed, investing this kind of status in epistemology is what we need to challenge at its very foundations.

Just look at the price we pay for the obsession and privileging of epistemology. Evangelicals in the Victorian generation in England lost many of their children and grandchildren to Roman Catholicism and agnosticism.[79] There are striking similarities between Protestantism in the nineteenth century in Europe and the situation in the United States today. Witness the extraordinary interest in the quest for the historical Jesus and the continued obsession with relating evangelism to social activism. Why did evangelicals lose their children in the nineteenth century? George Eliot (the pen name of May Ann Evans) certainly supplies a typical example of what went wrong. She was converted at the age of nineteen only to be deconverted three years later after reading Charles C. Hennell's *An Inquiry Concerning the Origin of Christianity* and David Strauss' *The Life of Jesus, Critically Examined*. She abandoned the faith, as Ian Bradley, notes, because Christianity "by emphasizing the will and acts of an omnipotent Deity... extinguished the possibilities of human love and service."[80] She gave up on God because she came to believe that the material content of scripture must be false. This undermined her vision of the authority of scripture. Earlier

---

[79] An especially insightful review of the situation in the nineteenth century in England can be found in Ian C. Bradley, *The Call to Seriousness: The Evangelical Impact on the Victorians* (New York: Macmillan, 1976).

[80] Ibid., 199.

in the nineteenth century John Henry Newman, converted to a robust Evangelical version of Christianity at the age of fifteen, had decamped to Rome after wandering from Evangelicalism through Liberal Protestantism to Anglo-Catholicism. We are not too far off the mark if we claim that he was looking for a way to safeguard the authority of scripture and its proper interpretation.[81] Protestants could not agree on what scripture says and were all too readily creating their own versions of Liberal Protestantism. Again epistemological issues were critical in his journey away from Evangelicalism.[82]

If I am partially right about this then Evangelicals clearly have a serious problem on their hands. So let me press the matter one stage further. Evangelicals have constantly lost their own precious children because they overcommitted themselves in their doctrine of scripture. They then paved the way for conversions to Roman Catholicism, for shifts into various Liberal or Radical forms of

[81] This is wonderfully visible in Tract 90.

[82] Note that I am not here reducing the worries that crop up to the epistemological, for much more is usually at stake, such as the validity of orders and sacraments. For a brilliant if tendentious review of Newman's life see Frank M. Turner, *John Henry Newman: The Challenge to Evangelical Religion* (New Haven: Yale University Press, 2002).

Protestantism, or for the outright embrace of agnosticism or atheism. They did so in the nineteenth century; and they are doing so today. It would be interesting to develop a list of scholars or church leaders who began as evangelicals or "fundamentalists" and abandoned it because of problems with the doctrine of scripture. Consider: John Hick, James Barr, Elaine Pagels, Robert Funk, Maurice Wiles, Bart Ehrman, and Bishop Spong. I have lost count of the folk I have met who have abandoned the evangelical tradition because of problems with scripture.

What is fascinating is that if they stay Christian the hallmarks of the Christian traditions they join are precisely the relevant epistemological commitments of the new group; indeed epistemology is constitutive of the identity of the alternatives. So let me put the matter simply: Evangelicals borrowed heavily from the epistemological bank at high interest rates, they then bet the store on a doctrine of the authority of scripture. When they lost the bet on scripture, their children and grandchildren have had to find ways to pay off the creditors. They had to look elsewhere for help. I propose that we cut off this exit by not making that bet in the first place.[83] So what should be done?

Getting a Fresh Handle on the Primacy of the Gospel

I think we need to find a better way into the future and it begins with the going back to the primacy of the gospel. We should begin with a clear and resounding acclamation of the good news of the gospel: God's kingdom has been inaugurated by the action of the Triune God who has sent his Son in the power of the Holy Spirit to deliver the world from evil. The Christian faith is not a theory of truth or knowledge; it is a victory gained by God in Christ for the salvation of the cosmos from bondage. It is a first-order network of robust indicatives; it is not a second-order schema of apologetics; much less is it a third-order account of how we should defend the first and second order moves we present to the world when challenged to give a reason for the hope that is within us. The church is not an extension of the philosophy department. Nor is she housed above their offices with elevators running up and down to a basement

---

[83] Note I am not claiming to prevent future exits; these will continue for a variety of reasons.

that sits on strong supporting pillars invented and installed by epistemologists. She is built on the gospel that is the power of God unto salvation made present by the Holy Spirit in conversion and exorcism and miracle evoked by the strong name of Jesus Christ.

To be sure, church teachers and leaders are free to develop whatever apologetic strategies and theories of knowledge they deem useful and expedient. There is no shortage of such material in the history of theology. Presently we are awash in a sea of such theories; we live in a time of excessive luxury; and those who teach philosophy and theology should be up to speed on them. However, to make such theories constitutive of the life of the church is to render us captive to philosophy. It is to take into the very brain cells of the church viruses that will eventually destroy the gospel from within. It will be a case of death at our own hands, by our own medicine. For once the ingested epistemology becomes obsolete, then the church becomes obsolete with it. Once the philosophers catch the flu, the faith or church that is dependent on them, will soon die of pneumonia. This dependence on philosophy is by far the best explanation for the paranoia in and around current disputes about foundationalism and postmodernity in evangelical circles. There has been a changing of the epistemological guards at the Evangelical Palaces. The old ones are retiring; and the new ones think that they have fancy new weapons to guard the palace and increase its evangelistic and political chances in a changing culture. We need a radical revolution: the guards need to be sent to the guardhouse, and the fate of the gospel should be taken out of their hands.

We can express this dramatically by insisting on three theses that I have developed at length elsewhere. [84] First, the canonical treasures of the church are not confined to scripture; they are constituted by a rich network of materials, practices, and persons. We need more than scripture to make us wise and build us up in the faith. We need the canonical practices of preaching, baptism, and Eucharist. We need the Creed to get our bearings intellectually in the new world of the kingdom and church that we have entered. We need proper icons to instruct the eye. We need the canonical theologians of the church to tutor us in real theology. We need the saints to inspire us to new levels of holiness. We need canons of discipline to protect us from smart Alecs and Alices and from devious activists

[84] See my *Canon and Criterion in Christian Theology*.

who insist on imposing their peculiar judgments and practices on the faithful by fair means and foul. We need proper episcopal oversight; we do not need more managers and party hacks, who have climbed their way up through the system; we need real teachers and saints, who love the faith of the church and know how to guard it and teach it with flair.

Second, the fundamental and primary purpose of the canonical treasures of the church are not epistemological but soteriological; they operate not as criteria or norms in epistemology but as instruments of the Holy Spirit to make us wise unto salvation and to equip us for service in the kingdom. The canons of the church are not epistemological canons to use in debates about epistemology; they are delicate and wonderful means of grace given by the Holy Spirit to equip the church to do the ministry of the gospel. Thus in handing over the Creed in baptism and confirmation we are not giving out propositional candy. We are making available the faith of the whole church that serves as a vital map for knowing who God is and for coming to terms with the mighty work of deliverance through Jesus Christ. This is not a matter of learning something by rote but of internalizing the very name of God in our hearts and minds so that we will know how to pray aright and how not to be fooled by silly substitutes. This handing over and its reception is not some prosaic exercise; it is utterly dependent on the secret work of the Holy Spirit in both teacher and taught.

Third, treating the treasures of the church as soteriological in character does not at all mean we give up on serious work in epistemology. As applied to scripture, it is clear that if we see scripture as mediating special divine revelation, then it is entirely proper to make appeal to scripture under that description. We can and should appeal to scripture in resolving theological disputes if we believe, as I do, that scripture gives us access to special revelation. However, it is important that we recognize the relevant shift of perspective. Furthermore, it is fruitful to read scripture as an important source of epistemological insight that deserves mining in our own day and generation. Scripture is full of epistemic suggestions that deserve extensive elaboration and reflection.[85] So in no way am I suggesting that we should abandon epistemology or even that we ignore

---

[85] For a foray into this arena on my part see "The Epistemology of Jesus: An Initial Investigation," in Paul K. Moser, ed., *Jesus and Philosophy, New Essays* (Cambridge: Cambridge University Press, 2009), 149-68.

appeals to scripture in theological disputation. But again, we need to know what we are doing; we need to recognize that we have shifted into epistemology and ensure that we pay the relevant price intellectually when we do so. At that point we have changed our ground. When we do so, we should not forget that divine revelation should be received first and foremost as a response to human sin rather than one more item to add to the list of topics we take up in epistemology. In its own way, revelation too belongs in one sense within the arena of catechesis.

A Backward Glance to the Origins of Systematic Theology

With this crucial work in catechesis in place, we can then get serious and excited once again about systematic theology. Here we should turn without apology to the founders of the discipline. In their case, say in Irenaeus, Origen, the Cappadocians, Augustine, or St. Symeon the New Theologian, there is next to no agreement in epistemology; on the contrary they were all over the map in this terrain. Yet they could still do their work. Why? It was so because they had an entirely different vision of what they were doing. And what were they doing? They were engaging in post-baptismal, university-level catechesis. Starting with those already converted, with folk who were initiated into the agreed faith of the Church, they sought to unpack, defend, articulate, and explore the whole New World that had been opened up in the gospel. Straining every intellectual nerve and using every tool at their disposal, they brought folk into a deeper knowledge of the God of creation and redemption. As Ellen Charry in her groundbreaking work has shown, theology fostered wisdom within the life of faith, leading the new convert into a deeper love for God and neighbor.[86] To modern and postmodern scholastics this orientation in theology looks limp and lacking in rigor; to those still caught on the epistemological merry-go-round it appears superficial and lacking in seriousness. All this, they say under their breath, is to be relegated to an extension of the Sunday school and to ascetic theology, while the real theologian gets on with deep, critical, academic theology. This is exactly the response we should expect from those who are committed to theological studies rather than to theology. It is real theology that we

---

[86] Ellen T. Charry, *By the Renewing of Your Minds: The Pastoral Function of Christian Doctrine* (New York: Oxford University Press, 1997).

need: serious discourse about the living God who has truly saved us from despair and evil and who has opened up for us in the faith of the Church a strange New World that not even the most brilliant among us will fathom this side of eternity.

Theology is first-order discourse about God; it is not one more interaction with what this or that learned scholar has written about God. Its goal is to deepen our knowledge and love of God. So when we offer up biblical and theological studies in its stead we are cheats and imposters. This is even more so when we turn theology into grand tomes on epistemology or extended discourses on this or that change in Western culture. To return to our main theme, the invention of biblical studies by theologians was a great moment in the history of Western ideas; but it was a wrong turn in the history of theology. Theology became a slave to historical investigation; over time she dug her own grave; she entered the darkness of Good Friday, and awaits her Easter resurrection. We need a resurrection into a new kind of systematic theology.

Speaking of Good Friday, let me venture a very brief illustration of what is at stake. Over the last few years I have been working on a book on terrorism and theology. With terrorism we meet a horrendous evil, the kind of evil that needs the genius of a Dostoevsky to capture in human language.[87] But how are we to handle this theologically? Certainly we need to think about such obvious questions as how the ordinary person, the state, the church, and its many victims might respond appropriately to terrorism. And certainly we should be interested in recent work in philosophy that tackles the conceptual and other issues that are in the neighborhood of terrorism. But what do we need to do to think about terrorism theologically? The initial challenge is simple: we need to look at terrorism as it figures in the life of Jesus. At his birth there was a terrible massacre of the innocents. Jesus lost his cousin to a brutal beheading carried out by a nasty king who was bewitched by a half-naked daughter-in-law, who was egged on by a nasty wife, who had a score to settle with one of God's prophets. Jesus himself went through a form of the death penalty that was designed to terrify both the prisoner and the crowds who saw it. Yet we are still only snatching the hem of the theological garment. For Christ himself is no ordinary figure in history; he is God

[87] His novel *Demons* is devoted to this topic.

himself in our midst; and we let loose our terror upon him. Yet through that horrendous evil, God has made plain both his mercy and his justice. It is that question, the question inside the faith of the church that should detain us and keep us awake at night. We need a serious account of atonement from this angle. And we then need to work through the full implications of what that means for a Christian response to terrorism. We will need more at this point than the sentimental and emotional talk about forgiveness that is currently the currency of theology. We need to figure out how to relate forgiveness to reconciliation, reconciliation to repentance, repentance to regeneration, and all of these to real justice rather than to the phony restorative justice beloved of celebrity archbishops from distant parts of the world. I realize I have put the matter very sharply and even polemically. And I certainly am not making a pitch for my own embryonic proposals, for there will be different ways to unpack the insights that will emerge. My aim is to awaken us all from our dogmatic slumbers and to encourage us to look again at the theological materials that have been cast aside so readily in the recent past.

Ironically, this shift of perspective leaves virtually everything as it is, where historical study is concerned. Historians are free to explore biblical texts, the history of Israelite religion, the emergence of the doctrine of the Trinity, and a thousand and one issues. They can even explore whether and how they might envisage biblical theologies. They can do so without the constraints that theologians sought to impose on them in the past. Perhaps the New Testament writers were merely functional Trinitarians; perhaps Paul was really a binatarian; perhaps Mark knows nothing of the virginal conception of Jesus. So be it. The deep convictions of the soteriologically oriented theologian are not undermined by such proposals. The great faith of the church is not so easily contradicted by such observations, as it would be, if we were still wedded to an epistemological conception of scripture. The Church did not simply commit herself to a canon of scripture, she also committed herself to a whole nexus of canons, that is, to a canonical heritage of scripture, saints, teachers, liturgical practice, creed, iconography, episcopacy, and the like. These were not grand norms of truth, justification, and knowledge; they were truly effective means of grace that, with the guidance and energy of the Holy Spirit, enabled vulnerable, fragile people to become saints and martyrs. So the theologian can relax and be flexible in how best to respond to the results of historical investigation. She can let the historian loose to understand the whole life of the church in all its maddening complexity and development. And there will be all sorts of ways to work out the cognitive dissonance this kind of work creates.

Of course, it need hardly be said that any historical work will rest on contested background beliefs, including theological and atheological beliefs, so the philosophical theologian will have plenty to say about the complex logic of historical explanation and judgment. We can be sure that many secularist historians will resist this observation, as they have done for generations, but the days of that kind of imperialism and intellectual intimidation are over.

No More Scorpions and Millstones

In the meantime the theologian need not wait to have a set of secure foundations; that whole topic needs to be addressed in the field of the epistemology of theology. True theologians have better and more interesting things to do. They are required before God to enable people who have entered into new life in Jesus Christ through the energy of the Holy Spirit to come to terms with the full riches of wisdom and life that have come to the world as an incomparable gift and challenge. To be sure, this will require them to play a host of roles akin to that of defense lawyer, medical doctor, inventive apologist, adept cartographer, sensitive prophet, ecclesial renewalist, and biblical exegete. Happily all this work can be done without first farming out the precious scriptures of the Church to biblical scholars, who may operate, according to the erratic contingencies of their guild, as functional atheists or as amateur epistemologists. Scripture will, of course, have its own inimitable place in the repertoire of resources deployed by the theologian; but it will not be their only resource; and it will function first and foremost soteriologically rather than epistemologically. At that point, those who come to theology looking for fish will no longer be given a scorpion. Hopefully too, Christ will have less use for those millstones that he warned should be used around the necks of those who caused his little ones to stumble.

Epilogue

Christianity can do little for civilisation till it is extirpating that egoism on which all civilisations play fantasies, and till it is absorbing civilisation in the kingdom of God. The Church as such need have little direct effect on current culture. It does not act on it by pressure. It brings no formulated answer to its problems, and no policy for its affairs. Its first condition is the new birth for a soul or a people, and its first work is to bring that to pass. All things else are added to that. All doctrine and organisation grew out of that. The light must come from the fire, not the fire from the light.

P.T. Forstyth[88]

Two Worries that Keep Recurring

Much of what I have argued in the foregoing has been taken up with technical questions that inevitably take front seat in the debate about what to do about the Bible in theology. This is as it should be, for theology is a serious subject that runs all the way from the bottom rung of Sunday School right up to doctoral studies in the top universities of the world. Yet the issues are not merely academic

---

[88] Forsyth, *Justification of God*, 276-7.

and technical; they are also spiritual and pastoral. Thus in the first lecture I lamented the fact that the outcome of the creation of biblical studies was the unintended loss of the gospel. This is clearly a spiritual issue of the first magnitude. In the second lecture, I was at pains to argue that the primary role of scripture is to make us wise where salvation is concerned. This too is a pastoral and spiritual matter of enormous importance. In my third lecture I argued that the drive to make theories of knowledge primary undercuts the primacy of the gospel in the life of the church, taking us back around to one of the crucial concerns of the first lecture.

However, I have found again and again that the kind of reorientation I am proposing can lead to acute spiritual disorientation if it is not handled with sensitivity and wisdom. Many think that the position I am advocating means that we should not care about how we ground our theological claims in a robust and fitting fashion. It seems to them to open the door to a kind of do-it-your-self vision of theology where anything goes. If scripture is not first and foremost the norm of theology, then we are left to wallow in a sea of subjectivism; this they feel will clearly be spiritually disastrous, for folk will lose their moorings and wander off into the wilderness theologically. So in

101

this brief epilogue I would like initially to address explicitly this pastoral and spiritual concern that will have cropped up in the mind of many readers. I shall then tackle the challenge of subjectivism.

The Pastoral Worry

At the outset let me say this categorically. If losing your current understanding of scripture will lead you to abandon your faith, then I would insist that you should absolutely hold on to the vision of scripture you currently embrace. From a Christian point of view, nothing is more disastrous than the loss of faith. So if your theory of the Bible is integral to your having faith in the first place, then stick to your theory. Do not move an inch unless you find a vision of scripture that in fact deepens and enriches your faith in Jesus Christ. I know many serious Christians (some are saints) whose faith would be wrecked, for example, if they came to believe that there was a single error in the Bible. This has been a common worry that shows up again and again in the history of the church. I understand it; and I fully understand the assumptions that undergird this worry. It would surely be spiritually suicidal to abandon the inerrancy of scripture if that leads

102

to a loss of faith. Hence, I repeat categorically that if abandoning the inerrancy of scripture leads to a loss of faith, do not abandon the inerrancy of scripture.

I would say equally categorically that if holding to the inerrancy of scripture leads you to lose your faith, then you should not hesitate to stick with your faith and look for a much better way to think of its nature and use. I know a host of believers who have abandoned their faith because they could not solve the intellectual and moral problems that plagued them when they took the text of scripture really seriously. Some of them reached the point where they hated whole books of the Bible; others became hopelessly distracted where the gospel was concerned. In either case they could not make any progress in coming to know and love God. What matters is coming to know and love God; theories of scripture are secondary and should be treated accordingly. So if your theory of the Bible gets in the way of knowing and love God, go find a better one.

The Worry of Subjectivism

These comments make it clear that pastoral and spiritual considerations are bedrock for me as a theologian, as a preacher, and as a teacher. I also want to make it clear that my proposals here in no way pave the way for subjectivism in theology; on the contrary they call for a rigorous defense of the Christian faith using the best resources available to us. This works needs to be conducted on at least two levels.

First, we need to draw on the recent work on epistemology that seeks to develop an apt way to think about how we actually gain knowledge in theology. There is no longer any excuse for the kind of sloppy work that one comes across among both students and professional theologians. For well over a generation Christians who work in philosophy have provided incredibly fruitful resources for tackling how we should best think of the rationality of Christian belief, how to deal with standard objections, and how to advance the discussion of both old and new challenges that are unfinished business. When I trained in philosophy in the late sixties the cupboard was bare. I had to fend for myself in a hostile world where philosophers ridiculed the truth of Christianity. At other times they made it clear that it did not even deserve to be a live option for anyone who wanted to take the life of the mind seriously. The situation has changed dramatically over the last fifty years. There has been a revolution in debates about the nature of knowledge and justification; there is now space for serious discussion about the rationality of Christian belief that was unthinkable in the first half of the twentieth century. This does not mean there are agreed upon answers; Christians have never agreed on how best to defend the truth of the faith. What matters is that we do in fact defend the truth of the gospel and the great doctrines of the church. We are in a much better position to do this now than we were at any time in the last five centuries.

Second, we need good popular works in apologetics that help ordinary believers keep their intellectual nerve when they confront their own doubts and when they run into hostile critics. There is nothing apologetic about apologetics. It is a hard-headed effort to display the rationality of the Christian faith, to deal with obvious criticisms, and to expose the flaws in the many intellectual alternatives that compete for our allegiance. In this respect the emergence of novel forms of hostile atheism and the arrival of Islam in the West are to be welcomed. The call, then, is for spirited popular works that are non-technical, accessible, and deeply persuasive. In this arena the work of C.S. Lewis has been unsurpassed in the twentieth century and continues to be extremely effective in our own day. Lewis was not a standard professional philosopher, but he had training in philosophy. In his day, there was little help available from within either philosophy or theology. This situation is changing in the academy; so we can surely hope that first-rate work in apologetics lies ahead of us in the next generation.

Within both the professional work to be done in epistemology and the more popular work required in apologetics, we will make little progress without a really hearty commitment to special revelation. God really does make himself known in creation and in conscience. God really has made himself known in the history of Israel and in the coming of Jesus Christ. God really has guided his people into the way of truth by speaking to them in radically diverse ways and in inspiring his people to gather up that truth in scripture, and more broadly in the canonical heritage of the church. This means that we will indeed turn to the Bible to ground our moral and theological claims. If we do so carefully, it is right and proper to speak of the revelation enshrined in scripture as a norm of truth; and from that we can readily even develop a fresh vision of the authority of scripture. Nothing I have argued here rules out such a move. What it does rule out is the effort to make any theory of this kind the primary description we deploy in thinking of scripture. If we want a word to capture the best way of thinking of scripture the right word is Wisdom. Why? Because this word draws us back into approaching scripture afresh on our knees and in repentance to be made wise unto salvation. Within this we can even think of the revelation enshrined in the Bible as central to mediating the Wisdom of God we so sorely need; here we bring revelation within the orbit of soteriology. We are liable to be led seriously astray when we reverse the relationship and, beginning with a vision of scripture as divine revelation, we then shoe-horn the offer of salvation into this orbit. Once we do that we are back in bondage to philosophy and we know all too well where that road ends; it ends in spiritual darkness and intellectual disarray. Whatever we do, the most important thing is to immerse ourselves in scripture in any and every way possible. It is scripture itself not theories about scripture that really make a difference in our lives and in the life of the church.

Immersion in scripture has been central to my own work as a theologian and a teacher. For over twenty years I have taught adult classes in my local church where I have exclusively focused on the reading and teaching of the Bible. I consider this work essential to my formation and survival as a theologian; and I know it is vital for the lives of those who attend these classes. Moreover, as a preacher I consider it my first responsibility to work from a meaty text or passage of scripture. Sharing the Wisdom of God in scripture, week in and week out, is not an option; it is absolutely indispensable for genuine growth in grace. The loss of the Bible in so many of our churches in the West is a scandal that needs to be corrected. There will be no lasting renewal of Christian faith and practice without a recovery of the reading and study of scripture across the life of the church. We can all lament the ignorance of the Bible that abounds; but the solution to that ignorance is first and foremost the fresh immersion of ourselves in its content.

The Significance of Historical Investigation

It was once hoped that biblical studies would make available the great treasures of scripture to the church at large. Frankly, I have benefited enormously from what careful historical study of scripture has long since made available. Not for one minute would I want to go back to some kind of premodern mindset that would set aside the gains that have been made. However, the hopes invested in biblical studies have not been realized in that the fragmentation now so common in professional circles has left most folk confused when they turn to biblical scholars for help. It was also once hoped that the study of the Bible together would solve the central challenge that has to be faced in the search for organic unity of Christians. This too has turned out to be a complete illusion. The Bible is now used extensively as a warrant for the kind of diversity in unity that totally undercuts the noble agenda of organic unity. Where once church leaders hoped to see unity, they find their churches coming apart over issues of sexuality.

At one level my strategy is to go back behind the creation of biblical studies and recover a much more viable account of the Christian faith, including its disposition towards scripture. The agenda at this point is unapologetically retrievalist in orientation. We need to face up to the problems that we have created for ourselves and repair the serious damage that has been done. This will certainly mean learning to read the scriptures with our ancestors in the faith who readily came to them with their spiritual senses alert to the quest for salvation and the good news of the gospel. It is always a great joy to come across intelligent pastors and preachers of the past who open up the Bible in ways that are both intellectually honest and spiritually nourishing.[89] However, it would be silly to cast aside the crucial gains that have been made in understanding the context and content of scripture as a result of historical investigation. As biblical scholars come to terms with the crisis in their profession and as theologians lend a hand in writing theological commentaries on scripture, we may yet hope that even better resources will be made available in even the immediate future.

The standard objection to really penetrating historical study of scripture has generally been that historians must by the very nature of their profession read the Bible like any other book. Thus they cannot allow, say, for divine

---

[89] Of late I have rediscovered the amazing sermons of F. W. Robertson (1816-53), one of the truly great preachers of the nineteenth century. Robertson initially wanted to go into the army but providentially was offered a place to study at Oxford before he got called up by the military authorities. While his university career was far from stellar, he found time to commit to memory in both Greek and English the whole of the New Testament. He died prematurely after a remarkable pastorate in Brighton at the age of 37. His four volumes of Sermons are extraordinary in their spiritual perception and intelligence. His commentary on I and II Corinthians is equally nourishing. All are readily available with an internet search.

intervention in the world when they read their sources critically. Nor can they allow for any kind of inspiration that would privilege the place of the Bible in understanding reality. I decided to pursue further graduate studies in philosophy in part prompted by the intellectual challenge that this line of thinking championed. In the end I came to see that such assumptions were radically flawed. Our work as historians depends on the relevant vision of causality that we bring to our study of the past. If we are atheists or if, as theists, we think that God is not interested, say, in raising Jesus from the dead, then of course this will be reflected in our understanding and evaluation of the biblical text. However, we are simply fooling ourselves if we think we know in advance that God does not exist, or, that if God does exist, He is not interested in acting directly in the world. These are exactly the issues that are at stake when we read the Bible as given to us in the church. We have to face the music at this point rather than switch it off in the name of our prior prejudices and commitments. Hence it is simply false to say that we must rule out the possibility of divine action in history or in human experience when we immerse ourselves in scripture.

We can come at this from another angle in responding to the claim that we must approach the Bible like any other book. This claim too is false on its face. We do not read a text in mathematics in the same way that we read a great literary work. Just as we must approach different intellectual disciplines with apt forms of inquiry, so too do we approach different texts with apt forms of inquiry. This applies even to the way we approach different texts within the Bible. We do not read Job as if it were a comedy rather than a brilliant prose poem wrestling with the problem of suffering; and we do not read the Gospel of John as if it were the latest edition of the Wall Street Journal. The Gospel of John makes it abundantly clear that it was written so that we might believe that Jesus is the Christ, the Son of God, and that believing we might have life in his name (John 30: 31). We may begin reading the Bible casually as if it were just one more piece of ancient literature; this is fine. However, it would be odd to think that this is where we will still be after reading it carefully. The testimony of thousands is that it has changed their lives from top to bottom in ways that took them totally by surprise.

Back to Proper Piety

I have circled back around to the importance of spirituality and piety in our understanding of the Bible. As my reference to the Gospel of John makes clear, this book (and more generally the Bible as a whole) was written to bring us to God and to repair the effects of sin and rebellion in our hearts and lives. The Bible is not just one more book among others; so we should approach it in a way that is fitting and apt rather than imposing our own agendas on our reading and then claiming some kind of intellectual superiority over those who do not share our assumptions. We can legitimately approach it with the testimony of the church which canonized it, preserved it, and provided ample space for its study, using every useful tool at her disposal. The effort to drive a wedge between a theologically informed and spiritually sensitive study of scripture, on the one hand, and a critical, scholarly historical study of scripture, on the other, is a bogus enterprise.[90]

---

[90] For a splendid text that provides a fine introduction to the study of scripture see David R. Bauer and Robert A. Traina, *Inductive Bible Study: A Comprehensive Guide to the Practice of Hermeneutics* (Grand Rapids, MI: Baker Academic, 2011). Robert Traina (1921-2010) was a professor at Asbury Theological Seminary when I was a student there from 1970-73. He was the greatest teacher of scripture that I have ever encountered. He was also a saint. Traina did his doctoral work in systematic theology on the doctrine of the atonement; he had an ear and eye for the theological and spiritual nuances of the Bible that were

113

Perceptive readers will have glimpsed in these later comments an important epistemological insight. Just as reading a great novel involves reading it with, say, moral and human sensitivity, so does reading scripture involve reading it with spiritual sensitivity. We need to read the Bible utilizing the appropriate spiritual senses. We read it, asking the Holy Spirit to enlighten us and lead us into the truth about ourselves and about God. We seek the help of God because our spiritual senses are often hopelessly dull and marred by sin. Even as we read scripture in this way our spiritual senses are repaired; we develop a hearing ear and a seeing eye. As we follow up the full implications of this observation, we are once again marching into the arena of theory of knowledge. However, once again the ordering of our study is important. We begin by immersing ourselves in the Bible to get food for our souls and to find salvation. As

---

astonishing to meet in the flesh. His work has been picked up among others by Dr. Alan Meenan, a fellow-Irishman and friend, who came to Asbury Theological Seminary with me and then went on to pursue doctoral studies in Old Testament at Edinburgh and Yale. After a long stretch as a pastor in various local churches, he is now committed to sharing his years of research in the wake of Traina in a ministry called *The Word is Out*. It is readily accessible on the internet.

we proceed down this road, we find that our cognitive capacities are expanded and that we enter a world of knowledge deserving of the best epistemological skills we can muster. As with so much else in the Christian life, we seek first the kingdom of God and then find that a lot of other marvelous gifts are buried within it. Some of those gifts are epistemological; we should open these gifts in gratitude to the God who saves and heals our souls.

About the Author

Born in Northern Ireland in 1947, William J. Abraham currently teaches at Perkins School of Theology, Southern Methodist University in Dallas, Texas. Educated at Portora Royal School, Enniskillen and Queen's University, Belfast, Abraham went on to receive a Master of Divinity Degree from Asbury Theological Seminary in Wilmore, Kentucky, and a doctorate in Philosophy of Religion from the University of Oxford, England. In 2008 he was awarded the D.D (h.c.) from Asbury Theological Seminary.

Other books written by Professor Abraham that relate to the theme of this book include *The Divine Inspiration of Holy Scripture* (Oxford: Oxford University Press, 1981); *Divine Revelation and the Limits of Historical Criticism* (Oxford: Oxford University Press, 1982); *Canon and Criterion in Christian Theology: From the Fathers to Feminism* (Oxford: Clarendon Press, 1998); and *Crossing the Threshold of Divine Revelation* (Grand Rapids, Mich: Eerdmans Pub, 2006).